Mother to Mother

Mother to Mother

Navigating motherhood through the generations

Rosie Kelly Smith

SEVEN DIALS

First published in Great Britain in 2026 by Seven Dials,
an imprint of The Orion Publishing Group Ltd
Carmelite House, 50 Victoria Embankment
London EC4Y 0DZ

An Hachette UK Company

The authorised representative in the EEA is Hachette Ireland, 8 Castlecourt Centre, Dublin 15, D15 XTP3, Ireland (email: info@hbgi.ie)

1 3 5 7 9 10 8 6 4 2

Copyright © Rosie Kelly Smith 2026

All photographs courtesy of the author

The moral right of Rosie Kelly Smith to be identified as the author of this work has been asserted in accordance with the Copyright, Designs and Patents Act of 1988.

All rights reserved. No part of this publication may be reproduced, stored in a retrieval system, or transmitted in any form or by any means, electronic, mechanical, photocopying, recording, or otherwise, without the prior permission of both the copyright owner and the above publisher of this book.

A CIP catalogue record for this book is available from the British Library.

ISBN (Hardback) 978 1 39963473 1
ISBN (Ebook) 978 1 39963476 2
ISBN (Audio) 978 1 39963478 6

Typeset by Born Group
Printed and bound in Great Britain by Clays Ltd, Elcograf S.p.A.

www.orionbooks.co.uk

For Billie, my Mum and my Granny

Contents

Introduction: A Hand to Hold	1
Chapter 1: Change is Inevitable	9
Chapter 2: You're Glowing	27
Chapter 3: Your Time is Still Your Own	41
Chapter 4: Every Birth is a Real Birth	55
Chapter 5: Everything is Temporary	73
Chapter 6: Fed is Best	93
Chapter 7: Every Baby is Different	111
Chapter 8: You Won't Create Bad Habits by Responding to Your Baby's Needs	125
Chapter 9: Sleep When You Can	139
Chapter 10: Do What Works For You	153
Chapter 11: Let the Baby Lead You	177
Chapter 12: Love Watching Them Grow	191
Chapter 13: It Gets Better and Better	213
Conclusion: Finding Your Village	223
For My Daughter	229
For My Mum	233
I Wish I'd Known . . .	237
Acknowledgements	241

Introduction
A Hand to Hold

When I first found out I was pregnant, there were a million things racing through my mind – and this was just the beginning. I not only had nine months to prepare for the birth, but a lifetime of parenting ahead too.

Whenever I went anywhere pregnant, and then when I went anywhere with Billie, I found that everyone – no matter who they were – had advice to offer on motherhood. Thankfully for me, the most common piece of advice I was given was to trust my gut – but I had no idea what I was doing and there was no gut to trust in!

I have a lot of friends with babies, some who are planning on having them, and some friends who just don't want them. The ones who don't have them yet and those who have decided it's not for them oddly say the same thing: how much they're not ready yet, and how much their lives will change. The theme of both conversations is the amount of pressure they've put on themselves. I felt this pressure too, before I knew I was going to have a baby. 'I *need* to get a house sorted, I *need* to have a successful job, I *need* to be in a certain state of health – physically and mentally.' There's a huge amount of pressure on women when it comes to motherhood, which has really increased over the last few generations, and it's so easy to become overwhelmed by everything we're told we need in place, alongside what we're told is the ever-ticking time bomb of our body clocks.

The minute I found out I was going to have a baby, all of the pressures of what life *should* be like to bring a child into the world just went away. Life didn't feel like it was going to stop; it felt like it was going to have a lot more purpose.

Very quickly though, I found myself overwhelmed by the mass of information that exists on motherhood today. You can feel, like I did, that you are kind of on your own when it comes to 'the right way' to approach parenthood. Looking to newspapers, magazines and social media, the amount of noise and conflicting information was enough to make me want to crawl into a hole and never even entertain the idea of having kids. The list of what parents are expected to do is growing by the day, and new mums can often feel pressured into making certain decisions around how they give birth or feed their child. It's so easy to feel like you're failing, and that's the feeling that has driven me to write this book.

Steve and I were lucky to get pregnant so quickly, but with all the excitement came the phrases, bits of advice and general sayings. We got the classics like 'They didn't do it like that in my day', 'Sleep when the baby sleeps', 'You're making a rod for your own back', 'You'll spoil them if you do that'. It's so easy for these common sayings to make you feel like a failure.

A Hand to Hold

What I really needed was a sane voice to get rid of all that noise, and just tell me what advice was actually useful! In this book, I look into where these phrases come from and flip them on their heads – because, after all, you can *never* spoil a baby.

In the first few weeks of Billie's life, it was as if all the books, information from classes and every leaflet I was given by the hospital was completely forgotten. What I needed was someone to talk to – and to have them listen. I spent less time scrolling social media and stopped googling everything, and ended up messaging my mum, my mum friends and my incredible midwife (who was there from the beginning). What I learnt pretty quickly was that you always go back to a mother.

In *Mother to Mother*, I wanted to create something which stored pieces of good advice (and rewrote the bad) in one place. I wanted to put into the world something comforting, but also as honest as possible – with not only my own personal experiences, but also those of the mothers around me. A hand to hold yours through the whole process. From talking to my mum, her mum and my friends who are mums, I wanted to find out what still holds up as useful advice, and what we need to reframe for new parents today.

Having Billie means that, in my family, we now have three generations of mothers who have had girls. Billie is what sparked the idea to create a book of wisdom across the generations, alongside my experience of a big shift in my relationship with my mum. I became much closer to her, and I also saw her relationship with her mum in a different light.

MOTHER TO MOTHER

Our approach to motherhood has changed so much over the years, with new gadgets and sleep coaches, it made me wonder how did my granny, or my great-granny, cope? And the thing is, they did! So, instead of turning to a new voice, I wondered if we should revisit the knowledge and support that has been passed down instead.

My granny's name is Anne King McMahon, and she was born in Glasgow on 22 September 1941. She was sent to a convent with her older sisters, Helen and Josephine, and her younger sister, Patzi, when she was 11. It was tough. The nuns were strict and the girls had to wear an uncomfortable uniform and clean the home for their bed and board. They went back to my granny's mother, Margaret, when they had families of their own.

Margaret (Granny Mac), also known as Peggy, was a formidable woman from Coldstream in the Borders, who trained as a chef. She was a very intelligent, well-read woman who would have gone on to higher education if she had lived now, but back in the 1920s, if you were a poor female, it wasn't possible. She had eight children who lived and one child, Sandy, who died young from scarlet fever, which was not unusual back then. She split up with her husband, John, who worked as a waiter, but he still went to her house for his dinner. It was an unhappy and quite violent marriage. Until he left, she was regularly beaten up, but she still visited his grave every year on the anniversary of his death. My appalled great-uncle Jimmy would watch her pour half a bottle of whisky onto his grave!

Out of all the siblings, I, of course, know Anne, my granny, and Josephine, my great-aunt. Like the McMahons, the

Kellys are originally from Ireland, and left there for Scotland to find work and a better life, as they were poor and working class. The Kellys lived in the Gorbals and the McMahons in Dennistoun – both impoverished parts of Glasgow.

My granny met my grandad when they were teenagers and got pregnant, and then married shortly after. She had to stop working when the pregnancy started to show, so there wasn't a lot of money coming in, just my grandad's wages. He was working as an apprentice, fixing televisions. I always make the joke that it was inevitable my mum would be on TV, based on what her dad did. He was a grafter and worked long hours overtime to earn as much money as he could. They rented a 'single end' in Ballater Street in the Gorbals (just one room with a sink and a small cooker in the corner, and a recess in the wall for a bed). There was an outside toilet shared by the whole building, or 'close', as it's called in Glasgow.

They got married at the registry office in Martha Street in Glasgow in July 1959, and went back to that tiny one room for a cup of tea and a Penguin biscuit. Sadly, the single end got broken into and all of their wedding presents were stolen – not a great start to married life! But they didn't have long to dwell on it, as my mum was born shortly after. When my mum was a toddler, they moved to Bridgeton, also in the east end of Glasgow, to a tenement flat (a room and kitchen) with an inside toilet and one bedroom, which my mum shared with her parents. Then her brother, my uncle, Graham, was born in 1965. My mum remembers how cool her parents were, with her mum listening to Dusty Springfield, The Beatles, Bob Dylan and sixties Motown classics on the radiogram, and wearing miniskirts and black eyeliner.

Mum's dad was promoted, and her mum worked as a Saturday girl in the tights department in Fraser's in Glasgow for a bit of extra cash, so they were comparatively well-off.

Mum and her brother were well fed, well dressed and taught to read and write before they went to primary school. Granny never taught Mum to cook; she would always insist Mum did her homework while she made the tea. My grandparents wanted the best for their children, and for them both to have a chance of a good education and a decent career. They weren't ambitious or pushy, but my mum knew they wanted to have that photo on the mantelpiece of their kids on their graduation day from university. My mum eventually gave up her place studying Russian at uni for a job on the local newspaper, *The East Kilbride News*, when she left school at seventeen (the same age her mum found out she was pregnant with her). They did get their framed picture on the mantelpiece when Graham graduated from the University of Edinburgh, and they got one of Mum when she got her honorary degree from the University of Dundee in 2013. They have one of me now, too!

My mum went on to work as Scottish correspondent for TV-am, joining in 1984 from BBC Scotland. A year later, she met my dad, who was a cameraman, and although she knew right away that he was 'the one', they were friends for a year before she wore him down. She hadn't really thought about having children until after they got married in 1992, by which time they were both approaching their mid-thirties.

A Hand to Hold

My granny had my mum when she was only eighteen (by some miracle, as she married my grandad in July and my mum was born in September. I'll let you do the maths on that one!). I think the smaller age gap between my mum and granny meant that they've grown up together, in a way. It also meant that when my mum had me in her early thirties, my granny was in her fifties and able to see me grow up – in a way which would have been completely different to how she was brought up, and how she brought up my mum. I was born in England, with Granny living up in Scotland, and that distance must have felt like another world. When Granny had my mum, all her family were either living on the same street or nearby. Every Sunday they would have lunch together, and there was always someone to talk to.

My mum wasn't able to do any antenatal classes or baby sensory classes like I did, because she was either working or sleeping when they were on. Granny wasn't able to pop over when I was born, but she and my grandad did fly down whenever they could. I was incredibly lucky that my mum was only an hour away from me when I was pregnant and, although she joked about moving in and sleeping in the bath, I was all for it.

Pregnancy, birth and the first year of being a mum is, of course, difficult – and everyone's experience is different – but that doesn't mean there aren't universal truths we can all learn together. What I most want to do is start a brave, honest conversation about motherhood and how you learn to trust your gut and your intuition. You may be reading this well after having your own child, and are even a grandparent now! This is a space for you, too.

At the end of the book, there is a list of things I'd wish I'd known, advice and resources that helped me.

So, please join me, and really use this book however you'd like. Write in it, circle, underline and highlight anything you want that makes you feel heard. That, for me, is the whole point.

1
'Life will never be the same!'
Change is Inevitable

I first saw this phrase written in a social media post from a company selling some sort of baby product I absolutely didn't need. My initial reaction at the time was excitement – I was pregnant now, of course life would never be the same! It was only later in the day that I started to feel like that phrase had the potential to make anyone feel a bit uneasy . . . Your life is going to change so drastically, there's no coming back?!

When my mum started telling people she was pregnant, there were a lot of congratulations and 'life is going to change', but always in a positive way. She never got people saying to save up on sleep, because she was already having to get up early for her job and so was used to no sleep. Another thing she never had to deal with was hearing other people's horror stories of birth, because, at the time, none of her friends had had babies!

Change started for me as soon as I found out I was pregnant. There were a few physical symptoms I had before doing the test (I was a few days late and had a weird metallic taste in my mouth), but the main symptom I had was worry.

My partner, Steve, and I hadn't been together that long at all before I got pregnant, but we both knew that this was it – we were the ones for each other. I think this was mainly because we'd both had serious relationships before and had both felt those relationships weren't what we wanted. We spoke about how we wanted children about five months into dating – not the idea of us having them together, but having them in general. It's such a huge thing that you need to be on the same page with your partner. I'm always baffled by couples who are together for years, even decades, and then get married and discover that one of them never wanted to have kids and the other desperately does. It's not a given, and is a huge life decision, so it's something you need to be talking about, I feel.

I wouldn't have dreamt of having this kind of conversation with previous boyfriends so early on, but it just felt right talking about big life stuff with Steve. It brought up the topic of my own body clock. We were both twenty-nine when we started dating, which is still seen as young these days, but, of course, that hasn't always been the case.

Being completely honest, I had no idea how easy or difficult it would be to get pregnant. With my own history and the media around women's fertility generally being very doom and gloom, I was under the impression it might not happen for us. Around eight years before, when I was twenty-one and in my final year of university, I had what I thought at the time was appendicitis but turned out to be a ruptured ovarian cyst. I remember waking up in the night with a really

Change is Inevitable

sharp pain on my left side, and after calling 111 I was told to go to A&E. This was my first real experience of the world of women's care in the UK, and it's something that has always stayed with me. My scan was in the same department as the maternity ward and I went with my dad. The nurse at the desk asked how far along I was, and I had to explain I wasn't pregnant. I couldn't help but think of those trying to get pregnant being in the same waiting room as women getting their first, second or third scans to see their babies.

With the amount of fluid that came out of me (this is just the beginning of a lot of detail, so prepare for that going ahead with the rest of the book!), the doctor and I were surprised to see that the cyst was still intact in the scan, inside my left ovary. I had to get surgery to remove it, and luckily they didn't have to take out the ovary, but it did leave it a lot smaller than the right one. After a few tests, it was 'declared' as a borderline cyst, and I was told I'd have to have another surgery to take tissue from other areas just to make sure that nothing horrible was going on. Luckily for me it wasn't, but I was advised to get a scan every six months and have a hysterectomy at forty, or when I was done having kids. At the time, forty seemed like a lifetime away, but as I got older and saw that people were having kids a lot older, it was always something I knew I needed to be upfront about when I met the right person. Forty was my cut-off, and felt like a ticking time bomb for me. And then I found Steve.

Steve and I met on a dating app and, after chatting for over a month, we finally met up. I always have a go at him now because I was the one who messaged first and asked for his number. Our first date wasn't perfect, but it wasn't awful! We were just trying to figure each other out as we went from talking on WhatsApp to real life. I'd made him come from South London to North London on a Tuesday night, as it was the only time before I went on holiday I'd be able to actually meet him. There was a lot of chat, but I just kept thinking that he wasn't really into it. It turned out that he was thinking *I* wasn't interested. I took a screenshot of the message he sent me the next day which read: 'Fancy another date, or shall we just leave it there?' I was convinced he didn't like me, but I thought, why not give it another chance? Thank God we both did. It turned out that he had also taken a screenshot of my message to him where he'd said, 'Thanks for a nice night,' and my reply read: 'Hope you got home safe.' So we were both as bad as each other.

For our second date, he organised crazy golf. I'd just come from filming so was covered in 'TV make-up', which just feels like layers of foundation on your skin. I remember him saying I looked nice and then, instead of taking a compliment (like most women), I said something about how I normally don't have this much on, but I had been with Mary Berry all day. I wanted to tell him who my mum was, but I wanted it to just come up in conversation – like, 'What do your parents do?' but once I'd name-dropped the best baker in the world, it kind of dawned on me that we'd have to talk about it. We'd been speaking for a while now, and I knew he wouldn't make a big deal about it, which is exactly what happened when I told him.

After that, and after he came to my flat-warming on his own and met everyone he could in one go, I knew

Change is Inevitable

we were in it for the long haul, and we needed to have the talk about having children. Steve and I both had the attitude that we might as well think about it now because it could take us a long time, or not happen at all. I knew that if I couldn't have a baby I'd look into adoption, but, of course, that process takes years. We didn't tell anyone that we had even spoken about kids or were 'trying', which I think meant that when we did tell people I was pregnant, they were nearly as surprised as we were.

I'm very conscious of the fact that my mum will read this, so: because we didn't know if I could have children, we wanted to start trying, and we weren't super careful. There, all done. You can open your eyes again now, Mum.

After around two months, I'd noticed I was two days late. I'd just got back from a trip to Scotland to see Granny, with an impromptu dinner in Edinburgh and a boozy night out with my best friend, Amber. When I was there, I had the start of shingles, and a horrible metallic taste in my mouth. I knew something was up, but didn't even let myself think that it could be the start of pregnancy. The night I got home, I remember waking up with night sweats, which I'd never had before, but that I put down to me wearing thick pyjamas, ones I wear all the time in the depths of winter.

I'd got home the day before New Year's Eve, and on the day, Steve and I decided we just wanted a quiet one. I was going to introduce him to the Scottish coverage of Edinburgh's famous Hogmanay on STV. Earlier that day, we went to do the food shop, and while I was there I bought a pregnancy test. Just to rule it out.

MOTHER TO MOTHER

I waited a while to do the whole peeing-on-the-stick thing until I just thought, 'Let's get it over and done with.' So, there I was in the loo, thinking I'd have three minutes to gather my thoughts before it said positive or negative. Those three minutes were a myth for me, as within seconds two blue lines came up. Steve was in the living room setting up the charcuterie board and all the soft cheese leftover from Christmas. After taking a minute to myself, I called him in, and he didn't even need to look at the test. He just said, with a smile, 'No way.' I wish I had recorded the moment, as it's something I'd love to look back on. It ended up being the best New Year's Eve I've ever had. We weren't in a sweaty bar trying to get a drink, but on the sofa talking about how this year would actually be different. So, life really was going to change, from that moment on.

A few days later, Steve gave his landlord a month's notice that he was moving out, and he used those weeks to move his stuff into mine. Aside from how I was feeling, the changes had already started with the fact that I now had a new roommate. I'd bought my flat and renovated it just for me, but in some way I think I knew there would one day be a baby there. I'm calling it a sign, but the builder didn't really properly think through the built-in wardrobe in what would become Billie's room. It wasn't deep enough, so the only hangers that fit were kids' ones.

My mum found out she was pregnant the same way I did – her period was late. She took a test early on and she was totally on her own. My dad was in the North Sea filming for Greenpeace and she waited until he came back to tell him in person. There was no FaceTime then and,

Change is Inevitable

because he was so remote, there was only a satellite phone that didn't get signal anyway.

She had no idea what to expect, and hadn't been around any babies, but they knew they wanted a family. The closest thing she had was her baby brother, who came along when she was six. When she got the presenting job at TV-am, Craig Millar took over her job as the Scottish correspondent. He had three babies under five (can you imagine?) with his wife Jacqueline, who was a massive help to my mum by reassuring her. (I grew up with their three girls, and two of them have become mums as well. I asked Claire, the middle daughter, for help, and Jennifer, the youngest, who had her daughter a few months after I had Billie, was soon asking for my tips. I didn't feel qualified to share at all, but it's so funny how we all matched in this way.) My mum knew things were going to change when she became a mum, but she could never have imagined the scale of it. Nothing can prepare you for it. It's really the first time you experience unconditional love.

My granny, on the other hand, didn't have the joy of finding out she was having a baby like my mum and I did. She only clocked that she was pregnant when she noticed that she was getting bigger and when she went to her mother's house with my grandad, when she was about four months pregnant. Granny Mac took one look at her and knew right away. Granny Mac wanted her to go to Cheltenham, to my mum's aunty, Jacqueline's, to have the baby and then put it up for adoption, but Grandad stood up for both of them and said no, they were getting married. Granny Mac forbade Helen, Josephine and Patzi from going to the wedding. She didn't go either. She was not a kind woman and, being completely honest, I'm not that devastated I never got to know her.

Three days after I found out I was pregnant, I made an appointment with my GP and, as luck would have it, she was pregnant also, which immediately put me at ease. I was expecting to have to do a pregnancy test to prove to her I wasn't making it up, but instead it was more of a short chat about the pregnancy: if it was planned, which hospital I should go to for the birth, signing up for a community midwife, and what I could and couldn't now do in terms of food, drink and exercise. I already felt like I was doing something wrong when she asked what prenatal vitamins I was taking. It had only been three days since I'd found out, and I'd wanted to ask a doctor about the ones I should be taking rather than being confused by lots of different opinions on social media.

We spoke about the best way to handle the medications I was on, as, for the past two years, I had been on sertraline for anxiety and had recently switched to antidepressants. Everything came to a head for me a year or so after the pandemic (it had nothing to do with that time, but it's just a good reference now for so many people). I was always a worrier. My first memory of it is ingrained in my head. I remember going to the PE field at school, where parents or nannies would have to come to pick us up, rather than the school gates. I was convinced no one was coming to get me. That's not a reflection on my mum and dad, but I just had it in my head I hadn't told them where I was. The school obviously had, and I was never forgotten about, but it was little things like that which seem silly but can just snowball. Every party I've gone to, I've always thought no one wants me there, and every job I've had, I would think they'd find out I was a fraud and sack me. After being away for nearly four years in Singapore working in and marketing for airlines, nightclubs and restaurants, I was ready to come home, but I was basically kicked out because I was made redundant and didn't have a visa anymore. Daily life just got a bit unbearable (when you're worrying and then crying because you're worrying), so I went to the GP, but he was reluctant to put me on any medication as he'd never met me before, so he suggested I go down the route of therapy first. Two weeks into that and I had a prescription for sertraline that I took alongside the rest of those sessions, and then I stayed on it. That was in 2021. I didn't like taking pills in general, which I think I get from my granny. Whenever she gets sick or even a headache, she won't take a paracetamol. I think it's a Kelly thing.

After what felt like a very short twenty minutes chatting with my GP that day, off I went with some leaflets. There was no peeing in a cup, no blood tests, no blood pressure taken. I felt a bit cheated by the whole first appointment process, as I wanted the pregnancy to be officially confirmed, and to know every appointment date going forward. My mind was buzzing with a million thoughts and questions, and I could understand why people find it so hard to wait for three months for a scan. Many people get an early one privately, which I ended up doing too. For me, it offered a lot of reassurance, but it's definitely something that wasn't on offer for my mum or granny.

MOTHER TO MOTHER

My granny only ever had two doctor's appointments in her entire pregnancy. In the fifties, there were no scans, and even though that would have been normal then, I can't imagine not knowing anything, really, about how my pregnancy was progressing. It's not just the lack of scans that is a stark reminder of how there was an entirely different approach to women's healthcare a generation or two ago. I remember my great-aunt Josephine telling me that when she went to her first doctor's appointment, both she and her doctor were smoking! My mum had more appointments and two scans in the early nineties with me, but nothing compared to what I've experienced.

When I asked Granny about going to her appointments, she said that it was the time when doctors mainly did house calls. The only one she really remembers was having to have an examination towards the end of her pregnancy. The doctor said he would need to see her vagina, and she didn't know what that was! I was on a call with my mum too when Granny said this, and we all burst out laughing. She said that no one spoke about sex or periods, and she only knew she was pregnant because she was getting a belly. After we'd finished laughing, I realised how heartbreaking it was to have lived in a time when women's health wasn't just ignored, but completely silenced. There was nothing about sexual health taught at school like we have now, and she remembers at the time everyone else her age getting pregnant too. It was just what people did.

The last question I asked my GP was whether I could tell my mum . . . If 'Bless you' could be captured in a single look, that's what I got back. There is no rule that you have to wait the full twelve weeks before announcing your pregnancy. Steve wanted to wait a while before telling anyone at all. I was happy to wait, with the exception of my parents.

I found those first three months so incredibly lonely, because the only place I could go for advice was the internet and social media (which is really not a healthy place to lurk at the best of times), when I so desperately wanted to call up my friends who had babies and ask if it was normal to feel sick constantly, rather than just in the morning, which was what I had heard in films. I think the early stages of pregnancy are when you need the most support. With zero energy, nausea, hormones flying all over the place, I was so lucky to not be working in an office. I'd taken the plunge of leaving a job that was going nowhere and had decided to try freelancing before finding out I was pregnant. This meant I was at home and able to nap whenever I wanted to. I genuinely don't know how others do it if you have to be in an office every day.

I made it to nine weeks of avoiding my mum because Steve and I wanted to wait until the first scan before telling our parents. One of the times I saw her before telling her was a spa day, and I had to make some excuse about just having had a pedicure so I couldn't go in the hot tub. I was also going on Mum's first leg of her book tour to Scotland, and knew I wouldn't be able to keep a secret like that when we were together so intensely for those few days, and I also wouldn't want to be seen as lazy for not being able to carry my own suitcases or all the books for the signings. I also think she just would have known something was up because I wouldn't have been inhaling black pudding, haggis or proper smoked salmon while I was there! The constant feeling of sickness was also now in full effect.

There was no way I was going to get my dad on the M4 to London unless there were multiple reasons to do so – his last trip was paired with going to a football match and some handyman work at the flat, as we didn't have a drill at the time. I did try to get him to come in for lunch with Mum, and mentioned needing help putting up a painting, but I knew that it was a long shot. Instead, I asked Mum to come to the flat after work. Steve was with me as we sat on the sofa and, once I'd stopped crying (Mum must have thought something awful was going on), I was able to tell her that we were going to have a baby. There was a bit of me that thought she already knew. In between Christmas and New Year, we went up to Glasgow to see Granny and I complained about everything tasting like metal, had tampons in the hotel's bathroom that were never opened, and had shingles. I knew Mum was going to be happy, but there was this nagging feeling in the back of my head that she might say something about how Steve and I had not been together that long, and how we weren't married – or even engaged. I really didn't need to worry at all.

After more crying and my mum jumping up and down, we then needed to decide what to do with Dad. He hates being out of the loop, so we thought we'd just video-call him and see if he'd pick up. He was having lunch with one of his friends, and I remember saying that we'd call him back when he was on his own, but it was too late – he knew something was up and had to be notified immediately. He scurried away on his own and didn't actually say anything for a good thirty seconds after I had told him and Mum had shouted 'Grandad, Grandad' repeatedly at the camera. Half a minute doesn't seem like a long time, but when someone is staring into space and no one's saying anything, it feels like a lifetime. He was obviously shocked, but very happy and did say that he would now have to buy a flat cap.

After we'd calmed down, I asked Mum how she had found out she was pregnant and told her mum she was going to be a granny. She said that she just didn't feel right in herself and was on her own when she went to the doctors, as dad was away bobbing about on a boat filming in the North Sea. She had a metallic taste in her mouth whenever she ate anything, and her boobs were sore, so the doctor made her do a test, which was positive. I couldn't believe that she sat with the news by herself for a whole week before telling my dad when he came home.

Telling people in person is something I would definitely recommend, and we really did try to do this with as many of our family and close friends as possible. We told my mum's parents between the Glasgow and Edinburgh nights of Mum's book tour. Granny had not been well for the past year or so and had never really been ill before. Mentally she's totally with it, but physically, she's just now an old lady. We showed them a picture of the scan, and Granny knew exactly what was going on. Grandad kept asking whose baby it was and looking at my mum!

The day after we told Mum and Dad, I went for the private early scan, just to make sure everything was viable and OK. The place that came up first on my search list was a clinic in Harley Street, and I remember thinking, 'How posh!'

Right before I went into the room, I had a sudden feeling of worry – what if something was wrong? The doctor said it might have to be an internal exam depending on what she could see, but that we'd try the 'old-fashioned' way first. For the past eight years, I've had these internal scans to check for cysts, and always thought one day I'll be getting one for the lovely reason of seeing a baby. I then had another wave of worry when she said the things she'd be looking for – where the pregnancy was (if it was ectopic), and if it was just the one. *Just the one.* Twins were not something I'd even thought about, and of course we would be so lucky to have two babies – but, my God, I needed to just get my head around the one for now.

The relief washed over when I saw this very small circle appear on the screen in front of me. The very small circle then started to move, and the doctor said I was going to have my hands full. She could also tell where the egg had been released from – my left ovary, which, unbelievably, was the one that was operated on. I got a couple of pictures printed off so I could show my granny, but it didn't resemble much – more like a wee piglet. I still had gel all over my belly when the assistant came in with a card machine, but for the peace of mind of telling our immediate family, I definitely felt like it was worth it. The scan was definitely a big moment for me; I realised change really was coming, in the best way possible.

Telling friends was something I also desperately wanted to do in person. My life was going to change, but so was theirs, in a way. I think this is an aspect of 'your life is going to change' that people perhaps don't talk about enough. Two of my best friends that I've known for way over ten years lived in Edinburgh, so at the same time as telling my grandparents, I wanted to tell them too. I was just a few weeks shy of the proper 'twelve weeks, you can tell who you like' stage, but this was my chance to tell them in person.

I knew there would be a scene with Amber. I started crying as soon as I saw her, which I know is awful because she must have thought something bad was happening! I then managed to ask if she remembered that the last time I saw her, we were a bottle of wine in and I'd just realised I was three days late. It then clicked and she started crying too.

I've known Jen since school, and I met up with her at one of Mum's book talks. Right before my mum was about to speak, I said I had something to tell her and before I could say anything, she looked at my bottle of water and said, 'Are you drinking that because you're pregnant?' When I said yes, she didn't believe me – I then showed her the scan, and she still didn't believe me. She said that the name at the top of the scan wasn't mine. Once I'd explained that it was the doctor's name, and mine was on the back, the tears started again.

While I was up in Scotland, Steve told his family. He'd asked them to go for lunch, which immediately put them on high alert that something was going on. He knew that there may have been a scene of tears at a restaurant so decided a video call before with a picture of the scan was the sensible idea.

Telling our family and friends was the thing that made me the happiest, but also made me feel weirdly quite sad, as the protective bubble Steve and I had built in those few weeks when only we knew was gone. I think this feeling

– of happiness tinged with sadness – is a common theme in pregnancy, and definitely something that keeps reappearing.

When I told friends who already had babies (who I've watched grow up), that gave me the green light to start asking them a million questions. I started to see them in a totally different light, and felt like a really bad friend for not being as supportive as I could when they were pregnant. I remember gifting one soon-to-be mum a candle because I wanted her to have something for herself, as everything else bought would be for the baby. I look back on that now and think how ridiculous I was. The thought was there, but I think I could have gone with some essential oils or something for postpartum recovery, rather than a three-wick lavender fire hazard!

Something I've learnt the hard way when giving people big life news is that you do find out who your real, proper, 'lifer' friends are. The people I've been friends with the longest were absolutely thrilled for us, but there were also friends who I thought I was incredibly close with who just didn't pick up the phone when I couldn't tell them in person, or who changed the subject within literal seconds of me saying I was having a baby. I'm not trying to say that you should get pregnant to find out who your real friends are . . . There are better ways!

The quietness after telling some friends was really telling. This huge, brilliant, beautiful thing that is happening to you and your family is also something that people have big opinions about. I think what upset me the most was that I felt like some friends felt they could no longer talk to me. I wasn't going to be able to go out drinking, or book a last-minute holiday, or, apparently, ever have fun again, so what was the point? With some friends, it was as if I was being cast as a 'stereotypical mum', who doesn't talk about anything other than nappies, and every conversation needs to be about boobs, sick or poo. I found that some friends who were at very different life stages drifted away.

Of course, we should celebrate every kind of life win, not just getting engaged, married or having a baby. Starting a business, doing a degree, moving house or leaving a toxic relationship are all causes for celebration, but society just hasn't quite caught up with that yet. On the flip side, I also don't see how if you want to meet someone and have a family, that that isn't cause for celebration too. Any good friends should be happy for you.

So, now our closest people knew the news, the changes had begun.

One night during my pregnancy, Mum stayed with us overnight, and just as we were lying on the sofa, right before going to sleep, I felt my baby move for the first time. It felt like a bubble bursting for me, not the butterflies that everyone had said, but it was another lovely moment for Mum to be there for and, I think, the first time she realised that things were going to change forever too.

2

'You don't look pregnant'
You're Glowing

The first time someone commented on my body, I was on the first nursery tour I'd organised, which also happened to be on the same day as our twenty-week scan. I showed up and there was another mum there already, who told me she was four months pregnant. When I told her I was five months, she gave me a look and said that I wasn't showing five months. This really did annoy me. The days of just touching someone's belly may be dwindling, but commenting on how big and small people are is still very much happening.

Was I too small for the stage I was at? Was something wrong? Was the baby not growing? All these thoughts then entered my head. I knew I had a scan in a few hours to check everything was OK, but if I hadn't had a comment like that, I wouldn't have been sent spiralling. My mum never had anyone say she didn't look pregnant. She was 'an Easter egg on legs'! Whatever the woman's intention was, her comment on my size felt so unnecessary, and I just wondered why she felt the need to say anything at what was meant to be a nice tour of the nursery!

I was under the impression I'd be doing the tour on my own, and it turned out that the other mum-to-be had actually got the date wrong (baby brain is real), but it worked out perfectly because she asked all the questions I hadn't even thought about. Just as those questions were being answered, I felt a wave of sickness and, after ten minutes of it, I asked if I could sit down. It was mortifying! The staff were so sweet and got me a glass of water in a plastic baby cup and a seat in one of the comedy tiny chairs. Up until this point, I was always just feeling nauseous – I hadn't actually been sick. The next thing I know, I'm in the children's loo throwing up into a tiny toilet, while I can hear the other woman on the tour being told about nap times. *Why now?* I thought. *After all the days in the house, near my own loo, why does this have to happen here?* Luckily, the sickness passed. Everyone told me that if you feel sick but aren't actually being sick, it's a boy. If you've been sick, then you're having a girl . . . Another old tale we're told!

A few months earlier, before the twelve-week scan, I had my first community midwife appointment in the local community centre. I knew to expect some tests but didn't really know which ones would take place, as the building felt more like a library than any kind of healthcare centre or hospital. I thought that I'd maybe got the location wrong, which was just the start of my worrying! Steve was working, so I went on my own with a list of questions I had written on the notes app in my phone.

You're Glowing

All was fine when the midwife, Laura, came and got me from reception. She was an incredible woman whom I immediately trusted. The first thing she said to me after I sat down was how terrified I looked, and we both started laughing. She went through everything to expect in the first trimester, and touched a little bit on the birth and how I had three options: hospital with midwives, hospital with a doctor or at home. This was my first decision made. I knew even before I thought about having kids of my own that I needed to be in a medical facility surrounded by every kind of drug if I was going to give birth.

My mum had wanted the same. The whole idea of 'breathing your baby out' wasn't trendy in the nineties, and she hadn't heard of anything like a birth plan. She wanted the safest option, ideally with her numb from the waist down, as God intended. Before the medication kicked in when she was giving birth to me, she had a bath and a TENS machine to take the edge off at home. When she was in labour in the hospital, she described her contractions as being like period cramps times a million, and remembers standing looking out the window and shaking in pain. There was a cute painting on the wall of three little mice, but when she was given pethidine, they turned into monsters with red eyes and fangs dripping with blood. Nowadays, pethidine isn't really recommended in the late stages of labour, due to the potential side effects for the baby, like drowsiness and affecting their first feed, as it passes through to them from the placenta.

For my granny, what pain relief you wanted and even what kind of birth you wanted wasn't talked about. You were just told what was going to happen to you. She was in hospital for a whole week (she loved that), and my mum was only brought in for feeds. (After my second night in hospital, one of the midwives asked what I was still doing there!) Like mine and Steve's experience, the midwives and nurses helped Granny to learn to breastfeed, showed her how to wash my mum and change her nappy with the massive pins. All the babies slept together in a room full of cribs at night, all yowling and crying.

My mum worked right through until two weeks before I was born. Weirdly, for someone who researches everything, she didn't read any books or watch any videos about pregnancy or birth, or even talk to her mum very much about it either. There was less information back then, and it seemed that there was an unwritten code about not wanting to make pregnant women afraid of the experience by telling them horror stories, or of all the things that could potentially go wrong. When I was born, my mum says she had an overwhelming rush of wanting to protect me, and a feeling of sheer adoration. She remembers I was a tiny, red-faced, squashed little angel with enormous eyes and a shock of black hair. Billie didn't open her eyes until the morning after her birth, one at a time. Like Billie, I didn't make any noise until I was getting weighed, and then I think both me and Mum must have thought we'd given birth to miniature banshees.

Before the twenty-week scan, and in the first few weeks of pregnancy, I researched everything. I decided to make three lists: things I can do, things I can't do, things there's not enough research on (so, basically, can't do).

You're Glowing

We'd booked a holiday for our joint thirtieths before *the news*, and I was planning on getting a spray tan before – cue the googling beginning. (I added it to my list of 'not enough research', by the way. The issue is that the effects of inhaling the spray are not known. I've since found an amazing natural tan, but it does make you think that if you shouldn't use a product during pregnancy, should you be using it at all? I had the same thought with food for a while, but then I remembered how tasty sushi was!)

I made a pact with myself that after every appointment or scan, especially if it involved a needle, I would get myself a treat or do something nice. I also wanted to tick some things off my list that I wanted to do 'while I can', so I took the plunge and booked a solo ticket to the cinema. I've always wanted to go on my own, but was worried that people would judge me for not having any pals. I went to one of those posh cinemas where you can order food to your seat, and I took full advantage of being in total darkness, so I wasn't judged for ordering an entire pizza, sweet and salty popcorn and a huge Oreo milkshake. I had this very non-guilty feeling that I could just eat whatever I wanted, and I knew that even though I was fighting nausea and had zero energy, food was my happy place.

I have never been one of those people who have a flat stomach. My mum's always said to me 'it's the Kelly Belly', and that genetically we have 'a good leg' but our middle area has never been our strong point. This is something I will not be telling my baby about, as I think if you think something looks a certain way – especially negatively – then you'll automatically hate it. My algorithm on social media started to change a lot, with videos of mums in their third trimester doing squats at the gym, and getting their six-pack back weeks after giving birth. To me, that's nothing short of toxic, and something I wish I'd done sooner was unfollow lots of pages and report any type of damaging content so it would stop coming up for me. I don't think this kind of content helps anyone. If you're into fitness and would like to regain a certain level of it as soon as possible after giving birth, you go for it. If that's not something you're concerned about, I don't think you need to feel in any way pressurised. There's enough to be thinking about!

At this early stage, I only had two days where I couldn't actually get out of bed. Still, I have no idea how women manage with full-time work, or if they do it on their own. Steve was now known as Dobby the Elf to me, as he was doing everything around the house – I knew I'd feel sick prepping dinner, especially meat, but had no idea I'd also feel bad smelling laundry detergent! He really did do everything.

At the end of the first trimester came the moment that everyone told me was worth all of it: our official twelve-week scan. I was a bit worried that it wouldn't be as special or that the magic might not be there as I had already gone for a scan, but this was very different. Steve was with me, to start with, and it was also the first time we went to the hospital where the baby would be born, which made it feel more real. My granny had never been in hospital before she gave birth, there were no scans and, during her pregnancy, the doctor would just visit at home. My mum wasn't given the option of a tour of the maternity suites in her nearest hospital, and didn't go until the day I was born. After her waters broke at home and she headed to the hospital, she was put into a big room downstairs on her own, before being moved upstairs. She said that she couldn't get her bearings and I would have found this so unsettling.

During the first trimester, a lot of things happen *to* you. Your body can often feel like a vessel, and some people find it really hard to advocate for themselves – to express that they do exist, alongside their baby.

Another blood test was done before the scan, to look for signs of pre-eclampsia and Down syndrome. What continued with every scan was a sense of worry, right before the gel was squeezed on my stomach, about what I was going to see on the screen in front of me. The worry disappeared when we heard the baby's heartbeat. It wasn't for long, but it was enough to calm me down. Just like at the previous scan, the wee thing didn't want to stay still for the doctor to measure its length and have a proper look at the heart and brain. If this happens, they make you lift your hips up as if you're doing a pilates move and then shift from side to side to get the baby to move into a better position. We got our classic first ultrasound picture, and off we went. The difference in the scans from a couple of weeks before to now was phenomenal. The wee thing had gone from a gathering of tiny lumps to looking like an actual baby.

As time went on, I finally had more of a bump. The wobbly bloat became firm, and I definitely looked pregnant rather than like I'd had a big dinner. My mum had the same experience with me, and so did her mum with her.

MOTHER TO MOTHER

We all expected a beautifully round tummy we could show off, but it was more of a mass. My mum said she took the idea of eating for two as a personal crusade. She described herself as 'a piglet', and loved waddling around. The thing that we had in common was how we felt about seeing our bellies move. My mum remembers sitting in the bath when she was about eight months pregnant and watching my fist ripple across her belly. 'Comforting and slightly bizarre' is how she described it, which is how I found it when I looked down at my belly around the same stage to see my whole bump sticking out on one side. I could only draw the conclusion that Billie was sticking her bum out and having a really good nap.

Something I never experienced, but my mum did, was a vertical line of black hair right down the front of her belly. It wasn't a thick pelt – just like a line drawn with a black marker – but that must have felt a bit disconcerting. Believe it or not, that line is all down to hormones that increase melanin production, and, just like it did for my mum, it fades away on its own.

One thing my mum did notice when I was pregnant was how much maternity clothes have come along. Mum wore the most awful tent-like frocks with polka dots and big bows, as if you had to disguise the fact you were going to have a baby. If I couldn't find something I liked, or thought the maternity options were too frumpy, I would just buy any clothes I liked, a couple of sizes bigger. I think maternity clothing now is a lot more considerate of people wanting to keep their personal style, and not change into having to wear frumpy 'mum' outfits like Mum was forced to.

You're Glowing

Aside from my main bump, I was noticing other tiny bumps on my gums, as well as bleeding when I was brushing my teeth. I asked my friend who, by total coincidence, was pregnant at the same time as me, and she very nonchalantly said, 'Oh, yeah, that's one of the other things no one tells you about.' It was down to another hormonal change I didn't know about, so off I went to the dentist for an appointment with the hygienist. Something to remember before you book is that NHS dental care (and prescriptions) are free when you're pregnant, and for the twelve months after you've given birth – a useful thing to bear in mind.

My biggest panicked moment happened when I noticed changes in my boobs – my nipples in particular. I was having a day on the sofa, so it was a no-bra day, and before I went to bed, I took off my big jumper and thought I was growing mould. My nipples were green! I called Steve to come and look. He was, at first, as confused as I was, but then looked at my green jumper and after some googling*, it turned out that the Montgomery glands (which I had never heard of before) of my nipples had started to open, and the fibres from the inside of my jumper had, for want of a better phrase, latched on. I'd genuinely thought for a second that I was falling apart.

Thankfully, growing mould isn't usually one of the many changes your body goes through during pregnancy, but I

---

* Google isn't ideal for everything, I know, and nothing beats asking a medical professional, midwife or other mums, but sometimes it can offer reassurance for these more straightforward things!

do remember thinking that no one had told me your boobs could start leaking and getting ready this soon. From then on, the days of not wearing a bra ended, and the era of the breast pad began.

An incredibly popular discussion point for lots of people throughout pregnancy is the sex of their baby. I thought I was going to have a boy up until the twenty-week scan. Steve is one of three (with two boys), his dad is one of three boys, and his cousins are – you guessed it – three boys who have now got boys of their own. I had zero preference on what we were having, but desperately needed to know. It would make it more real for me, and I wanted to start thinking about who the wee thing would take after. I could see my dad with a boy, getting him a Dundee United kit, and my mum putting a girl in the same outfits I'd once worn.

My mum was convinced she was having a boy, just like I was. I'd heard all the old wives' tales of a low belly meaning a boy and a high belly meaning a girl, but my mum just remembers being round! My parents didn't find out what they were having until I arrived, and my dad thought I was a boy for a whole second after he saw the umbilical cord . . . Then there's the popular myth about cravings too: sweet for a girl, salty for a boy. Mum's cravings were red meat, specifically frozen burgers, and she also got my dad to go out in the middle of the night for tinned mandarin oranges in their own juice. They had to be the ones with juice, otherwise the whole trip was wasted . . . I was a mix; I wanted sweet and salty foods. I had made myself beef teriyaki and noodles one evening, and I remember eating one mouthful, then spitting it out and throwing the rest in the bin. I never knew that making something you think you're craving and it becoming vile was a thing. All I drank were virgin Bloody Marys, and all I ate were salt-and-vinegar crisps and Crunchy Nut Clusters. Another myth is that glowing skin means you are having a boy, because girls take all your beauty – although maybe I can agree with that one, because I was a lovely shade of grey.

Ultrasounds showing the sex of the baby became possible in the UK in the early 1980s, so my granny had no clue what she was having. My mum could have found out, but her and my dad wanted a surprise.

On our way to the hospital for the twenty-week 'gender scan', we were joking that we were on the way to see our boy. I, of course, had a mini panic about whether everything was going to be OK before the scan, but our baby was moving around loads again. I detected a Scottish accent from the ultrasound technician, so of course I had to ask where she was from and start a conversation. We told her that we thought it was a boy, but everyone else had told us it was a girl. She asked us if we wanted to know, which we did, and then told us that, actually, everyone else was right – it was a girl! I started crying and asking if she was sure, and I remember the look of pure shock on Steve's face.

Towards the end of the appointment, the lovely Scottish lady said that my placenta was low – this is called placenta praevia – but that it was nothing to worry about until later on in my pregnancy. 'Nothing to worry about' was, of course, my cue to worry. I asked her what it would mean in the long run, and she said that they would look at where it was at thirty-two weeks, and, if it still hadn't moved, I'd have to go for a caesarean section rather than a vaginal birth. The placenta being that low means that the cervix is completely covered (essentially, the baby can't get out the way it normally would). For nine in every ten women, the placenta will have moved into the upper part of the womb as you get bigger, and won't be blocking this opening by the time of birth. It affects about one in every 200 births,[†] which is why it's not something you need to think about until your third trimester – but that doesn't stop someone, especially someone pregnant for the first time, from constantly thinking about it.

I had to go back a week later to check on the heart, as the baby had been wriggling around too much. Even after hip-wiggling, a glass of water, a wee, and a walk up and down the hospital stairs, baby girl was not budging. Steve had a really important meeting on the date of the second appointment, so I decided to ask Mum to come with me to this scan. She immediately accepted before I could finish my sentence.

We were so lucky to have the same technician this time, and not only talked about the baby, but also all things Scotland. Moving away from home means that when I hear a Scottish accent, it's not just my ears that prick up; my entire body does, just like a meerkat. I have to speak to the person, find out where they're from, and if we know any of the same people. Thankfully, the wee thing behaved herself this time and I felt way more at ease. The technician got

---

[†] https://www.nhs.uk/pregnancy/labour-and-birth/what-happens/placenta-complications/

a good look at the heart, and I asked her to double-check that it was a girl because I was still not one hundred per cent convinced.

I did hear Mum have a slight breakdown in the loo after. She said to me later that it really brought home that this was really happening, and that her baby was having a baby. It didn't seem quite real until she saw the scan. I think because I'd had my cry at the last scan, I was much more composed . . .

3

~~'No baby yet?'~~

Your Time is Still Your Own

Time went by very slowly. Week by week, the baby was a new fruit or vegetable on our app, and at the halfway mark, the wee thing was a turnip. Or a neep, which is the correct term. I was getting bigger, but everyone said my bump was so neat – up until the last few weeks, when people, literally on the street, started telling me, 'Not long now.' It was always meant in a nice way, but the 'No baby yet?' question annoyed me so much. Obviously there's no baby, because a) it's not in my arms, b) I'm humungous and c) I still look like a person who sleeps.

My new obsession at this time was my sleeping belt. I can only describe it as two mini foam mattresses on one side, and then a transparent section in the middle, which makes it so much more comfortable to sleep on your side while pregnant. I looked ridiculous, and Steve said I resembled the 'Snorlax' Pokémon. I also had to have my long pregnancy pillow, which is just a huge sausage that our sausage dog Ruby was completely obsessed with. Steve said that as soon as the baby was out, he'd be chucking it through the window (the pillow, not the child).

The wee thing was properly kicking at this point, and I could even start to see my belly move. I thought this would be a good ice-breaker when it came to my parents meeting Steve's parents that same week. My dad really wanted to meet them before the baby came, and I knew they'd get along. My parents think they're ancient because Steve's parents are a good ten years younger than them. Steve's mum, Helen, was twenty-three when she had Steve, so she's a very young granny in today's world.

Steve is the eldest out of three, and his parents had a baby every World Cup. Our birthdays are just two weeks apart, so our mums were pregnant at the same time. My mum was doing a load of 6 a.m. through to 9 a.m. shifts on TV-am, so she was up for work at 3.30 a.m. She thought this was good preparation for the sleepless nights to come, but nothing can really prepare you. When I asked her about my birth, she told me that when she left for work on her last day, she thought she'd have a whole month to prepare before I arrived on the scene. Her plan was to nest-build for a fortnight, and then eat chocolate and watch old Bette Davis and Joan Crawford movies for the next two weeks. Those first fourteen days, there was a lot of catching up with all the shopping for essentials that she said she should have been doing months ago and getting the wee nursery all ready. Everyone always says that your first is generally more likely to be late, but maybe it's a Kelly thing, as me and my mum were both early, so she never got to watch any of those old movies.

Your Time is Still Your Own

The weekend after our parents met was the BAFTA TV Awards, where Mum was getting a Special Award for her outstanding contribution to TV and just generally being fabulous. I'd been to a few of these events with Mum before, but this time was different, because I didn't have to wear ridiculous Bridget Jones pants, and I could actually breathe out the entire night. I managed to sit in the audience for two and a half hours before I gave up and headed for a pee, which was a new record. The comedian Tom Allen came over with some champagne and asked if I wanted some, which made us giggle, and then asked if I'd like a cigarette instead, which made us laugh even more. My dad absolutely hates events like this, or anything that involves wearing a suit, making small talk, or eating what he describes as 'rubber chicken'. Just before it was time for the after-party and everything descended into chaos, we made a break for it, and I was in bed by 9 p.m. An insight into the future!

As I got bigger, the flat seemed to be getting smaller, with the amount of paraphernalia that was being added daily. Steve and I had started conversations about where we were going to live when the baby came. If we ever had another baby, Steve said we could get bunkbeds, but it was slowly becoming clear that we would need to move sooner rather than later. The biggest question we kept asking each other was where did we actually want to live. I was up for staying in London so our daughter could grow up in the city, but the other option was Scotland.

I do remember at some point my mum saying she'd get some dirt from Scotland and place it under the bed when the baby was born, so 'technically' she'd be Scottish. I went to secondary school in Dundee and university in Edinburgh, so I did most of my growing up in Scotland, and I think I always thought I'd end up back there at some point. I'd love my baby to have a wee Scottish accent and go through the same trauma that I did, experiencing Scottish country dancing in PE.

The option that wasn't even an option was to move outside of London to where my parents were, in Berkshire. It wouldn't feel like progressing at this point in our lives; in a way, it would feel a bit like just going back to what I knew and not starting something new for our family.

My plan was to get Steve up to Scotland as often as possible, so he'd then fall in love with it. Perhaps after a few years of being in London, and maybe before the wee one got to school, we'd get up the road? Steve had signed up to do the Edinburgh Marathon before finding out we were going to have a baby, so this was working in my favour. We'd been up about six months before for my best friend's wedding and he was treated to all the sights. At one point, I do remember him saying that we could just move there.

At my six-month check-up with my midwife, I asked if I could get a 'fit to fly' note for going up to Edinburgh that weekend to cheer Steve on. In my case, she said no, as she could see from my last scan notes that my placenta was low. There is a risk of bleeding and going into labour before your due date if you fly, and there's also the issue of not being near your GP or hospital in case something does happen. I thought about driving up to Scotland, but instead opted for a weekend of sorting some baby stuff, washing all the clothes and toys and having a last weekend of just me and our dog, Ruby. This was the first time I was told I couldn't do something because of my body, but I also know I was putting the baby first.

When Steve got back, it was time to do health admin and get my whooping cough vaccine sorted, and a test for gestational diabetes. I've always had a sweet tooth and was a bit worried that I'd have to completely change my diet. I had to go into the hospital and drink a raspberry-flavoured sugary drink before waiting an hour for a blood test. I assumed that it would be a finger-prick test, like how diabetics test their blood-sugar levels, but I was very wrong. It was a proper blood test that I wasn't prepared for – I bruise so easily and always get a rash from plasters too. I did feel quite sick after the drink, and luckily hadn't planned anything for the rest of the day, so I just went home for a nap and then Steve made me dinner. I think I can genuinely count on one hand the number of times I made us something to eat at this time – he was fully living up to his name of Dobby the Elf.

Tests like these are something my mum and definitely my granny never had to do, as they didn't exist then, so it was a new experience to tell them about. Technological advancements in healthcare have clearly separated my experience from my mum's, more than my mum's from my granny's, I think.

The time came for our birthday getaway, and I got my 'fit to fly' letter this time after a scan showed the placenta had started to move away from my cervix. Thank God, because we had arranged the trip to Spain so it was in between our birthdays and our families and friends were flying out too. We had three days by ourselves before everyone descended.

Going away with a bump was bizarre. All the normal holiday prep of getting new clothes, a tan and a wax was long gone. Poor Steve had to use his beard trimmer on my bits, as it had got to the point where I couldn't see past my belly button. He actually did a great job. I ended up loving not worrying about how my tummy looked, or not stressing about getting into a particular outfit for dinner after eating way too many tapas for lunch. It was the first time I'd gone away and not worried about what I was going to look like by the pool in a bikini, and to be honest being happy in my own skin was the best thing I found about being pregnant.

This holiday turned out to be even more surreal when Steve proposed. He did it on the first night, and I had absolutely no idea it was coming. He's a nervous flyer, so having to get to the airport early and him looking a bit sketchy in security didn't have me thinking something was up at all. Before we flew, on my actual birthday, he said that one of my gifts hadn't arrived yet, but hopefully would come before we went away. When we got back from dinner on the first night, we were sitting on the terrace just about to call it a night, when he got up and said that my last present had arrived, he'd brought it with him, and that he was going to grab it. He told me to stand up and close my eyes. I still hadn't twigged, but there was a slight thought in my head about how funny it would be if he proposed. I never thought he would actually be down on one knee when he told me to turn around.

Your Time is Still Your Own

We called our families, and I remember the phone being passed to Steve's younger brother, Simon, who said, 'I can't keep up!' If someone had said to me a year earlier that I'd be engaged and having a baby, I wouldn't have believed it.

When we got back home, it was time to really start getting ourselves prepared. I had spoken to a few friends about antenatal classes, and they had either not done them or said that it was only worth it to meet people. I had another friend who just decided to learn 'on the job'. I had done a ton of research and had so much support from my midwife and friends with babies that I felt OK without the classes, but Steve had a chat with someone at work who told him that it was worth doing. It couldn't hurt, right?

These classes were never a thing for my granny, and my mum couldn't ever make the morning classes in her area because of her shift pattern at work. She told me she felt very underprepared by not going to them, but she had the luxury of asking TV doctor Dr Hilary all her questions at any time!

Our classes were split up into four sessions in person and then four sessions online, which were Q&A video calls with midwives. The in-person sesssions were held in a room upstairs in a pub. It was during the Euros, so a pub might not have been the best venue, but the sound of the match going on downstairs was actually a welcome distraction from the video of a woman 'vocalising' her contractions.

I was a tiny bit confused that the hour had focused on vaginal birth and only the last ten minutes on C-section deliveries. At this point, that's the road we were going down, but I did think that everyone should know more about caesareans, because that might end up being what they had, whether it was planned or not. I'd made some notes already for my birth plan but when I asked my mum about hers, she just looked at me blankly. There was no point in even asking granny! Essentially, in your birth plan, you write down who you want in the room, whether you want a birthing pool, what pain relief you'd like access to (all of it), what you want to happen to the placenta, what position you want to be in, if you want delayed cord-clamping, and also if you want the baby to have regular checks or skin-to-skin first. I had done one birth plan for a vaginal birth and one for a C-section, which, after this first class, I made a ton more notes on.

At the end of the first class, we had what was essentially speed-dating to get to know the other mums- and dads-to-be. I got used to the same questions of: 'How far along are you?', 'Do you know what you're having?', 'Where do you live?' and 'How long have you been together?'. I remember leaving that first class and telling Steve how relieved I was that he had proposed the week before. Everyone else was very grown-up. The average age of women having kids in London is thirty-seven, and I had just turned thirty. We were both so nervous and it felt a little bit like starting a new school.

The next week we had a whole hour on hypnobirthing, which was a bit much. We had to wait until week three for the 'practical baby care', which was the one Steve was really wanting to tick off the list. He just needed to know how to change a nappy, and then he'd be fine. Those are his words. That week, we had a different midwife taking the class, and honestly it felt like being back in school. Instead of telling us how long we had to register the baby's birth, she set up a quiz to see who got the answers right first.

Baby first-aid was our last class – and, to be honest, the one that left me feeling more worried than any of the others about what was to come. Steve wiggled his way out of this one somehow, so I went by myself. There were tiny baby mannequins we had to pretend to save from choking, and a *Where's Wally?*-style game about what hazards may be in a nursery.

At the end of the hour, there was a tiny Q&A that focused on postpartum. It was literally about ten minutes, and I felt like it just glossed over how you might get depressed, what your body might look like, and what might happen when you got home. This felt like a huge topic we should be talking about for a whole session. Taking a baby home for the first time was an imminent experience for us all, so why weren't we talking about those first few weeks more? I'd noticed that – not just in these classes, but in general – the conversation with pregnant women is always about pregnancy and birth, and then it stops. There was barely anything about this new stage of life for the mum, yet this is when everything changes.

I was around thirty weeks when we got our nursery furniture delivered and started ordering some essential bits like wipes and nappies. Even though I had a low-risk pregnancy, having these bits in the house in case she came early was a huge relief. Steve built the bedside crib, the cot bed and the dresser in one weekend. I knew he wanted to get this all sorted, as his cousin's baby had arrived a few months before at just thirty-two weeks, and nothing was prepared.

I think it would be easy to feel as if, in these moments, no one is thinking about you. You're prepping for a new baby to arrive, a new phase of life, but it's easy to forget that you're still going through something huge. It's why whenever someone asked me, 'How's it looking, no baby yet?' I'd feel quite annoyed.

One of my last midwife appointments was to go through what you need in a hospital bag. So far, I had a suitcase that was cabin-size, and a big overnight bag. You can tell just from that sentence how overprepared I was, but, actually, it was just my anxiety taking over – at any point, I needed to be ready. My mum took a tiny bag with her when she had me, containing a tiny babygro, cardigan and blankie for me, with nappies and Sudocrem, a TENS machine, and a nightie, slippers, dressing gown, change of underwear and moisturiser for her. My granny had just focused on getting things ready at home, with everything she had bought from Lewis's on Argyle Street in Glasgow. She had a Moses basket, a mattress, a pillow and a sheet – all costing a grand total of eight pounds. Parents now can easily spend thousands on welcoming a baby.

Laura, the midwife, measured my belly as always, but said that compared to the last time, it had grown too quickly. I didn't know this could be an issue at all, as I thought it was kind of normal for your belly to get bigger. However, it can be a sign of gestational diabetes, so, even though I had already done the blood test with the sugary drink, it was back to the hospital for me to do it all over again.

Your Time is Still Your Own

While I was waiting to do the test at the hospital, I went through my entire hospital bag with a fine-tooth comb. I split it into three sections: one for me, one for the baby and the other for Steve. A few things that kept being mentioned by my friends who had been there and done it was the need for a long phone-charger cable, because the plugs are far away from the bed; lip balm, because your lips get so dry in hospitals; peppermint tea to help relieve wind after a section; and some sliders (absolutely not flip-flops) for walking about, as you'll be wearing some comedy compression socks and your legs will likely swell up from the surgery, too. One thing I had decided to do was go all-out. I got new skincare, all my favourite things, new comfy socks, and I brought my own silk pillowcase for extra comfort.

I remember one of the midwives looking at me like I was mad for bringing a massive tub of Vaseline that would last years. I'd seen a woman on social media saying that if you rub it on a baby's bum right after birth, you won't have to scrub meconium off later. The midwife said to not worry about stuff like that, and that other things would be on my mind, like trying to pee. Steve dealt with that first nappy and sticky, dark-green to black poo that would scare anyone if they didn't know about it.

I got the results of the blood test later that day, and everything was thankfully OK – our baby had just had a big growth spurt.

After my twenty-week scan and being told about the low-lying placenta, I had to plan for both a C-section and a vaginal birth. I think this is something everyone should do as, in 2022 and 23, over 21 per cent of all childbirths in England were emergency C-sections.*

Before the later scan at thirty-two weeks, which ended up being internal (where they shove a big wand up your bits), I was almost selfishly wanting them to tell me the placenta was still low, because then the decision would be made for me on what kind of birth experience I would have. I'm generally very indecisive. In the end, my placenta had moved, which is great news as it stopped any complications – even with a C-section, it can be a more complicated operation if the placenta isn't where it should be. At this point, I had four months of section research at my disposal, and I ended up deciding that having a C-section was what I wanted. Knowing I could control this version of the birth (even if she came early), and having thought this might be the outcome anyway for so long, it just felt right for me.

At this point, Gaviscon was becoming as essential as water to me, and I'd made a list of all the foods and drinks I needed to really avoid now. One weird thing that felt like heartburn to me was air fresheners. We had a new one in the car and a diffuser in the kitchen. Whenever I went in the car or walked into the kitchen, it was as if the liquid had been directly poured into my mouth. Vile. On top of the heartburn, I was dealing with sciatica on my right side, which my mum had also experienced when she was pregnant with me.

---

* https://www.statista.com/statistics/407706/method-of-birth-delivery-in-england/

Your Time is Still Your Own

I set up a group just with the mums from the classes we'd been to, so we could talk about our bits without being worried about the dad's reactions. We met up in a café, and it must have looked bizarre. There would have been around ten heavily pregnant women all sitting at one table, starting off a bit shy and getting louder and more comfortable with each other as time went on. We began by talking about what we were thinking for our births, and then we ended up talking about where we grew up, the worst weddings we'd been to, and the all-important question of what our first drink would be when we'd had the babies. Mine heavily depended on the weather and the time of day; I wanted an Aperol Spritz if it was sunny, a Bramble if there was rain, an Old Fashioned if it was cold, a Bloody Mary if it was in the morning, a gin and tonic if it was in the afternoon . . . I could go on. We'd each paid nearly 200 quid for the antenatal classes, just to have some friends, but it's the best money I've ever spent. I do know mums that chose not to do classes and just learnt on the job. Whether you do them or not, you will find a way to meet your village, and that's incredibly important.

4

~~'Too posh to push'~~
Every Birth is a Real Birth

However your baby comes into the world, the most important thing is that they are safe, and so are you. Women have been fighting for their freedom of choice forever, and how they give birth should be just that – their own choice. The right to pick a caesarean birth in England and Wales was only introduced as a new guideline in 2011 by the National Institute for Health and Clinical Excellence (NICE). I wasn't overly excited about either option, but because of my placenta praevia, it was something I'd thought a lot about and decided to stick with.

The media-conceived (no pun intended) 'too posh to push' line was used to describe Victoria Beckham when she welcomed her first child, Brooklyn, by an elective caesarean. She later spoke about it, saying that her doctors had told her it would be 'unsafe' for her to give birth vaginally. Instead of the birth of her first child being a celebration, the tabloids went with a different angle. A caesarean is major surgery, running the risk of infections, blood loss, organ damage and blood clots. For it to be trivialised as something women do as the easy way out is a narrative we have to get out of our heads. If anyone denies you having what you want, you have to find your voice and defend yourself. It's your right and if you do struggle with conflict or get any pushback from anyone – in the medical field or family or friends – remember that the choice on how you give birth is completely down to you.

As soon as I hit thirty-six weeks pregnant, it seems a Batman-esque signal went out to everyone I knew to message me to ask how I was. Our family and friends knew my due date, but I didn't expect people to have it in their calendars! It was around this time that we booked the C-section in – and we made the mistake of telling our family the date. She was going to be born on 29 August, which would be one day over thirty-nine weeks. With hindsight, I think I would have preferred to have fewer people knowing the exact date, to lessen the amount of communication we had to do during this time!

One thing I kept hearing about from all angles at this point was Braxton Hicks contractions. I thought I had them a few times during the night, but they were what felt like mini-contractions – not the tightness and pressure-like feeling that contractions actually were for me. I knew something was going on when we were at my parents' house one day, and I thought I was possibly going into labour. Steve's parents were there, as well as my mum, granny and her sister, my great-aunt Josephine.

My stomach felt tighter than it ever had before, and I thought I'd call the number my midwife told me to in case something was happening. This was the first time I had a bad experience with maternal healthcare, as the man I spoke to at the hospital kept asking me if I was in labour. I kept saying that I had never been in this situation before, so I didn't know, but that something was going on. He then kept repeating that if I came to the hospital I wouldn't be seen for hours, so instead I messaged my midwife. Even though it was the weekend, she thankfully got back to me and calmed me down. My main takeaway from the call was that I'd know if I was in labour.

This is something that can't be said for my granny! She didn't pick where she was going to give birth, or visit the maternity hospital in Rottenrow in Glasgow. On 30 November 1959, she had terrible stomach pains and took the trolley bus with my grandad to Dennistoun, and walked up the steep Whitehill Street to her mother. Having had so many children, her mother quickly realised that Granny was in labour, and got a taxi to the hospital in Glasgow. My mum was nearly born in the lift! Granny had zero pain relief and it all happened very quickly. She wasn't prepared, so didn't have a bag with her, but the hospital would have provided most things, apart from a nice nightie. Her mother left her, as women usually gave birth on their own, and back then dads weren't allowed anywhere near the birth. My grandad didn't meet his daughter until the next day, when my mum was all washed and fed with a clean nappy on.

After speaking to my midwife, I calmed down, but Steve was pacing up and down the garden, and we decided to go back to ours earlier to be nearer the hospital, just in case.

Little did I know he was back in surprise mode again. The day after we got back, he took me to a pub nearby, and when we walked in, the manager gave us a nod to go up the stairs. It was only then that I realised something was up.

Through a frosted glass door, I could hear laughter and walking into the room, I saw a bunch of my best friends in the corner with a huge 'Baby Shower' sign. I obviously burst into tears, but that was nothing compared to what happened when my bestest friend Amber turned up. She had come for the day from Edinburgh by train, and could only stay for two hours after travelling for much longer than that. I didn't know I wanted a shower until I had one. We played games, did a quiz that included a fact that surprised us all (babies aren't born with kneecaps!), and had to guess what the record was for the heaviest baby ever born. (If you ever need to know this, the answer is 22 pounds or 9.98 kg.) Once I'd stopped crying at how unbelievable my friends were, it was time to say goodbye to them, knowing that the next time I saw them it would be with a tiny person in tow.

Baby showers are quite modern and very American. My mum and granny had no such thing. My mum was given a Moses basket on a stand that was wrapped up to look like a motorbike on her last day of work. Everyone had cake and bubbles, and that was as close as she got to a shower. Two weeks before I was born, she had her own version, which I wish I also did. She sat and watched all the episodes of the original *Poldark* on DVD with her best friend from school, my Aunty Joyce, drinking tea and eating vast quantities of chocolate.

Every Birth is a Real Birth

I was two days away from hitting thirty-seven weeks, and my ankles were now cankles. I'd been feeling isolated and wished Steve was able to take more time off so we could both be twiddling our thumbs together. I'd noticed he had been doing his own version of nesting. My dad had been the same, concentrating on all the practical things before I was born. He got the nursery painted and decorated, the changing table and crib built, and the car seat sorted. They thought they were prepared, but none of us had a clue about how our lives would be completely turned upside down.

I kept getting sent links for fire extinguishers, carbon monoxide alarms, pressure washers and leaf blowers. The last two are apparently a necessity as the front of the house needs to be clear in case we fall when holding the baby . . . I said yes to most of these things, but did reach the point of putting my foot down when Steve started going through all the appliances in the house and saying we needed new ones. I've had the best rice cooker for the past two years, and Steve seemed to think it was going to burst into flames as a piece was missing (it was not). I learnt that he just needed me to say no, gather his thoughts for ten minutes, and then he would then realise we didn't need a new Nutribullet, as the blades definitely wouldn't just fly off.

I had my first unsolicited 'touching my bump' moment when I went to get my brows done. I book the same woman every time because she's amazing and never remembers that I'm a repeat customer. Halfway through, she asked me if I was having a girl (the very same conversation we'd had before) and I said yes, and told her how much the baby was wriggling. Then, all of a sudden, her hand was on my bump. I really didn't mind, because I knew her – I think it would have been a whole different story had this been the first time I'd ever met her. I found it sweet before remembering she didn't think she'd met me before, so perhaps does this to every pregnant person she sees. This was definitely a better experience than when a friend of mine knocked on my belly to 'get the baby to do a kick'. Safe to say, we're no longer that good friends.

We'd hit thirty-nine weeks, and our C-section was scheduled for 5 p.m. We checked in a few hours earlier, and as I'd been fasting since my pain au chocolat first thing in the morning, I think the hunger was distracting me from feeling any kind of panic. I even had a nap after the anaesthetist visited! Compared to how anxious I'd found myself during the birth prep, I was surprisingly very calm. Steve was given scrubs and, just before 5 p.m., we were told we were going to be waiting slightly longer, because there were a few emergency sections happening. I was calm, but both sets of parents were definitely not. We eventually went down to the baby floor at 7 p.m., and by that point, they were probably expecting the classic message of 'Mum and baby doing well.'

When it was finally go time, the midwife told Steve to take the wheeled cot down, prepped with baby's tiny hat and a nappy inside. To think that a human would be in there in a few hours was something neither of us could get our heads around. I'd seen women having C-sections in films, but it's always just the part where the baby comes out, never what actually happens before. I walked into this tiny room filled with people and the anaesthetist that had seen us earlier explained how he'd do the cannula here, and then everything else would happen in the theatre. He was incredible, but I did wonder if he was doing some reverse psychology when he said that the cannula would be the worst part and then everything after that was easy . . . I had to sit on the bed for the epidural and flop over like a banana. Steve took his role as DJ very seriously, and popped on some calming music. I got Hans Zimmer's *Interstellar* soundtrack for the epidural.

Just as it was all about to kick off and I had to lie down on the bed, all my very chill feelings went out the window, and I suddenly burst into tears. Steve had one of my hands and a lovely nurse had the other. I think I just needed to get it out of my system, because when I got Steve to switch the music to my birth playlist, I felt a lot calmer. You're expected to have classical music blaring, but I made a playlist that actually made me feel good. For me, that is 1970s and 1980s disco. Anita Ward's 'Ring my Bell' was the first song that played and, when I saw a couple of the nurses dancing, I started to relax a bit.

The anaesthetist explained that I wouldn't be able to feel anything, but would be able to feel my body moving. He had a tiny can of cold air and sprayed the side of my belly down to my hips, asking what I could feel. I knew I'd gone cold where he sprayed, but I couldn't feel the air on my skin. Totally bizarre, but a great way to explain what was happening.

My mum's experience was very different. I wasn't for coming out, so she had been given medication intravenously to help get things moving. She had an epidural at 8 p.m., but it only worked on one side of her body, so I did have it in my head that mine might not work too. Around 11 p.m., she was fully dilated and told not to push, but after such a long time, I came out in a rush. It meant my mum had to have a lot of stitches, but she was oblivious to what was going on down there. She said she felt a bit of pulling but not much pain, which reminded me of when I got one of my wisdom teeth taken out.

A few minutes after the anaesthetic, they said they were going to break my waters, and it honestly sounded like they had just burst a balloon with a very loud gushing noise. Just as Rod Stewart's 'Do Ya Think I'm Sexy?' was finishing up, and I was having a wee hum to myself, the anaesthetist casually said that he could see a head. I had no clue the show had begun! The screen was firmly up and Steve was by my head, not wanting to look in case he got freaked out by me being literally sawn in half. Totally by chance, Diana Ross's 'I'm Coming Out' started playing as the anaesthetist said he could see some shoulders. I had what felt like a long time to panic, because I couldn't hear any crying – but when it started, it didn't stop! They lowered the screen and there she was. Covered in gunk and screaming the house down. It was so surreal. I didn't have that immediate rush of love everyone talks about – that came the next morning, when I stood over her cot and had an overwhelming feeling of wanting to protect her. I weirdly compared it to the time when Steve proposed and I turned around to see him on one knee. I had no clue what was going on, basically!

She was quickly handed over to the midwife, who did some checks and asked if we had a name. Steve and I had decided that it was going to be Billie, but we had wanted

Every Birth is a Real Birth

to see her before setting it in stone. When the midwife asked, though, I said Billie without even thinking. My parents always told me that if I was a boy, I would have been called John, and they had a few girls' names that were coincidentally all flowers: Daisy, Poppy and Rosie. I thought my name meant something, but my dad picked Rosie because, when I was born, I had red cheeks. When we chose Billie, it was all down to just loving the name too!

Steve was with her while she got her weight checked and a vitamin K injection. She was then wrapped up and placed in Steve's arms, before going on my chest for our first cuddle. I don't know if it was because of the way she was lying, or the position I was in, but I could only have her on me for a bit before I started to feel incredibly nauseous. The magic anaesthetist shot some liquid into my cannula that he said would taste like onions. Within seconds, I felt better. While all this was going on, they were stitching me back up. Grace Jones, Earth, Wind & Fire and Kool & The Gang had had their greatest hits played in theatre by that point, and it was now time to head up to the recovery room and for me to finally get something to eat.

Now, my dream scenario would have been my waters breaking naturally, then going for a planned C-section, so I could have had that experience of my waters breaking. I remember saying to my friend that I felt like I might be missing out. She ended up having an emergency C-section after being in labour for forty-six hours, and assured me that I was not missing out at all!

You're always told that every birth is a real birth, and I knew this, but it still didn't sit well with me before I did give birth. What I think now is this: new mums are constantly facing certain expectations – from themselves, and others around them. It's hard not to think a certain way about the kind of experience you want, even when you're also being told that it's your choice, your body, your life. It made me think back to the antenatal classes I'd sat through, with only the last ten minutes out of an hour dedicated to C-sections. Everyone wants the same outcome – a healthy baby – so why aren't all the routes babies may take to get here spoken about as frequently as each other? That's why I've included mine as fully as possible here – just in case you're not familiar with the experience.

One thing I would change about my birth experience, though, is telling our families the exact time. Because the C-section time got pushed back, it meant messages relaying that the baby was here were sent a lot later, and I think both our mums were having kittens. I'd maybe even go one step further and give them a different day . . .

Once we got up to our room after the section, our midwife Leah put Billie on me to try breastfeeding. Although my milk wasn't going to come in for a few days, she was suckling away. It was completely surreal, and the first time 'mum intuition' had come into play. I remembered our twenty-seven week scan, where the doctor had pressed a button and bam! There she was in 4D on the screen. I could only see half of her, and the doctor had explained that the umbilical cord was in the middle of the screen and she was sucking on it. He printed the picture out for me to keep, but it looked a wee bit like something from the *Alien* films. We joked that we had a hungry baby on our hands. The minute Billie came out, she was screaming, and I remember thinking she was maybe hungry because of that. She was quiet after our midwife popped her pinkie finger in her mouth, and at that moment, seeing her simple fix, I thought, 'Great, I've got this, I know everything' . . . I don't think I could have been more wrong.

I had something to eat while she was on my chest, and it seemed like this would be how things would be: Steve would be feeding me, I'd be feeding Billie, she'd then go to sleep and that would be our cue to go to sleep, too. It was time for our midwife to go home and the night staff to take over. I adored Leah – she was so calm, and I wish she could have stayed with me the entire time. My mum's midwife was called Precious, and she stayed on after her shift for Mum's labour. There was a doctor that came in to see Mum the next day, who didn't introduce himself and just said, 'We're doing hips today,' and he was so rough when checking me. Mum asked the midwives afterwards what had happened, and their response was, 'He's very old-school.' We had a version of this test with a nurse who came in to check Billie's hearing and reflexes, which involved lifting her head and quickly releasing it in her cot. We were told exactly what was going to happen, and that, if she cried, it was just a good sign. It definitely seemed that there was more communication compared to when my mum had me.

That first night in hospital can only be described as completely mad. I was experiencing a weird mix of adrenaline from having just had a baby, alongside sheer exhaustion, both mentally and physically. Billie was, we'd predicted, a very hungry wee thing, and we'd brought formula with us so she could have this until I was ready to feed her. The midwives asked if I had stored any colostrum (the fancy name is 'colostrum harvesting'), and I hadn't because I was too scared to, which felt like my first failure. They said to express some now, and then they could feed her that too. I'd read that if you stimulate your breast milk to come in by hand, expressing the colostrum, it could put you into early labour because your body would think the baby had arrived and needed food. This was, of course, a load of rubbish, as I later found out, but at the time, it was easier to just do what I felt comfortable doing. You can start 'harvesting' at thirty-six weeks, and your midwife can give you the feeding syringes to take home. One big tip Laura gave me was not to buy the ones online that are not exactly for your nipples, because those ones are actually catered to vets!

Needless to say, I had no idea what I was doing, and the midwives very kindly offered to help. This is the one vivid memory I have from the hospital room – Billie being with her dad and me falling asleep, boobs completely out, with a midwife on each nipple squeezing away – for what, in the end, looked like a teaspoon of colostrum. It was sticky and yellow, and I remember thinking how amazing that this was coming out of me. After a good hour, they had filled up two syringes' worth, or 1 ml. I thought this would do Billie until my milk was in by day three, but nope. She had guzzled it in less than half the painstaking time it took to get it. I think this was the point the midwives looked at both Steve and I and said they'd take her for a few hours so we could get some rest. I was on morphine, paracetamol, ibuprofen and stool softeners (the glamour!)

every few hours, so I wasn't getting a chunk of sleep at a time, but for that first twenty-four hours I weirdly just felt so wired that the lack of sleep didn't really hit me until we got home. Steve, on the other hand, looked like a zombie the next morning.

Time didn't really exist here. Steve could have said it was 6 a.m. or 9 p.m., and I would have believed him. We both had agreed that when it came to visitors, we would see how we felt after the baby was born. We knew that if my mum hadn't already pitched a tent on the street, she would be coming. Steve's mum had said she wanted to come, of course, and if my mum was visiting, then it was only fair. I don't remember much, but she came, held Billie, got her photo, and then left. Very annoyingly, my parents were getting a new bed delivered and had to wait for that to happen before coming, so they got there at 7 p.m. This did, however, mean there was no granny overlap, so there wasn't a competition for cuddles! Funnily enough, it was my dad who came into the room first and made a beeline for Billie. I could see his eyes welling up, and once they'd both sat down, Steve passed her to my dad first. My mum was a lot more calm and collected than I thought she would be.

We stayed in hospital for another night because I wasn't feeling one hundred per cent. I didn't want more visitors and kind of thought that would be a no-brainer, but Steve's dad was desperate to meet Billie. It was only fair that he should come, as every other grandparent had met her, but I was in a bit of state at that point, with my boobs hanging out, a bag of wee hanging from the bed, and desperate to just rest. When Steve's dad arrived alongside his mum, they had a cuddle, got some pictures, his mum passed me some breast pads, which was so thoughtful, and then off they went without being told.

When Mum gave birth, in High Wycombe just outside of London, her parents were in Scotland and came to visit a week after I'd arrived. My grandad was in hospital and when Mum called him to say I'd arrived, he shuffled to the phone – and skipped back after hearing the news. Mum had my dad in hospital with her the whole time, and my Aunty Joyce was the first visitor. She wasn't an aunt by blood, but my mum's best friend from school. I hope everyone has an Aunty Joyce.

When I was pregnant, the biggest piece of advice my friends gave me was to do with visitors. They said to not make any promises, nor to have anyone round for at least a week. With me being an only child and so close to my parents, I had no issues at all with them both coming at any point. I do think that when it's the daughter who is having the baby, her parents are naturally going to be the alpha grandparents. My mum and dad were going to be the ones who would get the first Christmas, the first holiday, and would be the first babysitters for an evening or weekend away. I wanted my mum, and so she would naturally be the granny who would be doing way more of things like changing nappies, burping, playing and just generally looking after Billie if I needed a nap or wanted some time to myself.

Our first panic came on night two, after my parents had left and it was just the three of us. When Steve changed Billie, he saw her feet were purple, and this hadn't come up in any classes or reading I'd done. The midwife said it was completely normal, and just Billie's circulation coming to terms with being in the real world, but it was another unexpected surprise I wish I could have known about before.

Our plan was to have a two-night stay in the hospital and then go home on Saturday afternoon. I think having the C-section so late on the Thursday meant that, by Saturday morning, I was just not ready to leave. For me, this was when my anxiety really ramped up. I had been feeling it before, reading about what could happen during birth, but this was a whole new scale of worry. The hormone drop was something I wasn't prepared for, either. I don't know if it was completely physical, but, whenever I stood up to go for a walk, I felt so out of breath, and when I sat down, I then felt really dizzy. The midwife ordered an ECG as my heart rate was faster than she'd have liked. Everything came back normal and, after a visit from the consultant, who assured me I was OK, I felt comforted when she said she wasn't going to discharge me that day.

Steve went to get some air, so I was alone with Billie for the first time and, after a bit of a struggle, I was out of bed and leaning over her in her little plastic cot. She was sleeping, and so unbelievably beautiful. I couldn't get my head around the fact that she had come out of me, and the tears just would not stop.

When it was time to prepare to go home, we needed to get Billie ready to leave the hospital environment. I thought I had brought a lot of clothes – sleepsuits that would cover the wee thing's feet, sleeveless vests in case it was really hot, and long-sleeved vests. I was under the impression that vests were for if it was warm, and the sleepsuits were for if it was cold. But when it was time for her to get changed for the first time, the midwife helped Steve put a short-sleeved vest on first, and then a sleepsuit over it. Newborns need more layers and I felt like this was something I should have known about.

The time had come for the catheter to come out and, as much as I didn't really enjoy carrying a bag of wee down the ward on my walks, I secretly loved not having to go to the loo for a long time. I wasn't allowed to actually be discharged without doing a massive wee and measuring it in a very lovely cardboard bedpan. I thought my first attempt was quite impressive, but it wasn't good enough. There was a lot of blood in my pee, which I didn't know was a thing.

Another thing I didn't know was going to happen was the cramping. My uterus was shrinking, and it got worse when I was breastfeeding. My back at this point was in unbelievable pain, and I couldn't believe no one had warned me about how the energy is literally being sucked out of you.

My mum had made the choice to not know all that much beforehand, and I often wondered if I didn't know what I was in for, whether I'd have been able to deal with it better. Sometimes, when you dread something so much, you make it into a big deal. Even if you do all the research and watch all the videos, no birth goes to plan or is exactly what you think it will be. My mum wishes she'd known a bit more about breathing and relaxation, because it might have helped prevent her from getting all the stiches she needed, and feeling like it all happened so fast.

Every Birth is a Real Birth

There were lots of different midwives at the hospital, all of whom had completely different advice and suggestions. Everyone was very well meaning, but I just didn't know what to do or whose advice to follow. One asked me if I'd brought a bib, and I said that I was told not to bring one; another asked if I wanted to try pumping, but I didn't have one at that point. One midwife was shocked that I'd brought along my white fluffy slippers. More shocking than me bringing them was that I miraculously hadn't got any kind of bodily fluid on them at all. I'd gone for a size up in them because my feet were still so swollen, something I thought would go down right after the baby was out, but not yet!

I didn't know how different I would be physically, too. My boobs were huge, and so was my belly. I remember Princess Kate coming out of the Lindo Wing just after giving birth to Prince George and asking my mum why she still had a tummy. The idea of bouncing back and looking like nothing had happened was so normalised in our society. I now think how annoyed I would have been if someone had asked me to show my baby to the world hours after I'd just given birth.

It was time for a shower before heading home, and that's when I realised how immobile I was. I had to keep the door open just in case I fell over, and Steve was on guard in case someone saw my arse. I did have to call him in to help me put a comedy maternity pad on my pants, and also help me into my pants and my pyjama bottoms.

I was really ready to go home by now, and I think Steve had been ready after the first night. The anaesthetist came back to see us before we left, asking, 'What are you still doing here?' He was joking, but it did make me think how wild it was that just after being cut in half, I was expected to be on my way home with just some standard painkillers, plus a human being to keep alive.

Steve had decided he would go and get the car and park outside the hospital entrance. It meant I would be properly on my own with the baby, and I kept making conversation with the midwife so she wouldn't leave. The midwife took us to the lift, and that's when I started crying. By the time I made it to the car, though, they were happy tears. I'd felt like we'd been in that building for days, probably due to the lack of sleep and not really registering what time or even what day it was.

After the longest twenty minutes of my life in the back of the car, shouting at Steve to go even slower than five miles an hour over a speed bump, we had made it. We were finally home – together.

5

~~'Enjoy every minute, this is the easy bit'~~
Everything is Temporary

I was so looking forward to the 'newborn bubble'. The general consensus regarding this period is that your baby will never be this small again, and you'll never have this time again – when it just feels like it's really just the two of you in the whole world. I think this is why I felt even worse when I didn't love it, because the narrative around it had told me I should. Was I a bad mum if I didn't love every minute? Aside from recovering from birth and the hormone dips, there's a tiny person depending on you for absolutely everything – which, as lovely as it is, is also incredibly daunting. My friends with toddlers said to enjoy the baby not moving so you could get stuff done. In those first few weeks, though, nothing gets done. At one point, I wondered if I could nap in the shower while eating a sandwich.

I had heard stories from family and friends about the first night at home after giving birth; that it would be a dream and create a false sense of security about the upcoming weeks, months and years of Billie's childhood.

MOTHER TO MOTHER

We definitely didn't have this dreamlike experience. Billie had slept in her plastic cot in the hospital, so we were under the impression that she would be totally happy in the cot that was in our room, next to the bed, complete with its own rainbow sheets, a stuffed owl that played an array of music and white noise, and netted fabric on the sides. But no. It was not for her. It rocked and everything, but the movement only seemed to make her more upset. That first night, Steve and I took turns with whose chest she was on. We swapped every few hours. All the adrenaline from being in hospital had worn off, and I didn't think I'd ever been more exhausted. I had a great way of not falling asleep when she was in my arms though: putting my tongue between my teeth and waking myself up when I accidentally bit down on it.

Billie slept on her own during the day in her little sleeping pod on the sofa, but night was a completely different story. When light started to come through the windows that first morning, we decided to make a game plan for the next few nights. Steve likes a plan and although there was no real way of gauging what Billie would do, we decided to create shifts for both of us, so that we could each get guaranteed sleep. For the first couple of weeks, I slept from 8 p.m. to 10 p.m., then I'd be up with Billie until 1 a.m., sleep until 3 a.m., and then I'd have her until 7 a.m. Steve would then take her and I'd sleep until 11 a.m. Absolutely mental.

I mentioned this to my mum, and asked if she had tried sleep training or the idea of self-soothing for babies, and she had no clue what I was on about. Essentially, it refers to a process by which parents allow their babies to fall asleep independently by letting them cry it out. There are more gentle approaches, but that's it in a nutshell. She said the thought of me being upset was actually painful, so putting me in my cot and just leaving me wasn't something she ever considered. For my granny, my mum was put in her cot the night they got home from the hospital, and that's where she slept. Co-sleeping wasn't a thing for her at all, and having babies cry themselves to sleep was just what you did. She was a teenager when she had my mum, and she also had a very scary mum of her own telling her what to do. She felt like she didn't really have a say.

As I hope is already clear, and something I want to reiterate again as a defining part of my motherhood experience, is that I was – and still am – very much in the camp of doing what's right for you. I knew some mums had their babies in their cots from night one, in their own room, and some had their babies in their beds until they were two years old. I do really believe that if you put pressure on yourself surrounding the situation, you'll feel worse when it doesn't go to plan. If you haven't had children yet and are planning on doing so, the big spoiler is, babies really don't have a plan. I think this is why the simplicity of my granny's actions, leaving Mum to 'cry it out', meant that a generation of women like my granny just 'got on with it' – and didn't work themselves up around when the kids slept.

What's also interesting about sleep and babies is that a baby isn't going to fit in with you. In my experience, there's no logic to your baby's sleep, which is hard to get your head around. Once you realise that sleeping patterns are as individual as babies themselves, though, it does take the pressure off a bit.

For me, healing from surgery with no sleep made my recovery time longer. I was told it would take longer to get back on my feet compared to a vaginal birth, but I was so surprised in the hospital when I was told I needed to walk so soon after (and equally surprised that I could do it). There's also a little more you need to think about, such as blood-thinning injections. They aren't something I knew about before, but you have to use the injections for ten days after your C-section. Puncturing myself was not something I ever thought I'd be capable of doing. The first day at home, I was on my fourth injection, and the midwives that had done it in the hospital made it look so easy. The plan was for it to be Steve's job. The sides of my stomach had taken it in turns with getting stuck with a needle, and I'd had a bit of bruising come up, so we thought we'd do it in my thigh instead. This was his time to shine, but I must admit it didn't go well. He was too worried about hurting me. At one point, the needle was in and he asked if it was OK to now push the actual medicine in. From then on, I just did it myself! I realised how brave I actually was, and you will, too, even if you hate injections like me. This was something I didn't have a choice in, and it had to get done. I found that putting a bag of frozen peas on my tummy beforehand to numb the area made it easier.

You also have to wear massive maternity pads and huge disposable pants, which I really came to love. It was so easy to just whip them off and chuck them in the bin! One thing that did make the whole healing journey easier was my

Everything is Temporary

'Peri bottle' an upside-down easy-to-squeeze bottle with a long neck that shoots out water to clean your bits. Like a portable bidet. The glamour! For the first few weeks of being home, I couldn't really bend over without my insides hurting, so the logistics of going to the loo alongside the everyday task of wiping my bits was now something I had to think about. This upside-down squirty bottle skooshed out water that, I must say, felt not only cleansing, but very refreshing . . . Try it!

That first week, we had no visitors come in, but I was so lucky that my best friend lived around the corner. True friendships really do shine when you need them. He never actually came into the house, but he walked me up and down the street, delivered pasta, made his famous Malteser traybake and brought us bottles of water when our sink decided to fall apart on day six. (If you ever need a plumber round asap, say you have a newborn. However, the plumber did then end up being our first official baby visitor . . . Apart from what felt like hundreds of Amazon deliveries. No one tells you about the amount of cardboard that's accumulated and how much recycling you'll do when you have a baby.)

Our next visit came from my midwife, Laura, who needed to do the heel-prick test on Billie, as well as have a look at my stitches. Everything had been perfect with Billie in all the checks in the hospital, apart from her being a wee bit jaundiced. Her eyes were fine, but she looked like she'd been on a week's holiday. I don't know if it was because it was Laura doing the test, whom I completely trusted, but I felt so relaxed with her holding Billie, and she stopped crying and forgot about the tiny needle that had to go into her foot as soon as I fed her. It was very weird seeing her blood for the first time dotted all over this paper sheet.

When it was time for Laura to look at me, she was able to take out some of my stitches, but a few of them still had some time to go and were properly stuck to me. I also had a big bruise around the incision on my left side, which was where the surgeon would have cut first. I couldn't sleep on my side because of this, as it felt like I was being stabbed. Twisting over and picking Billie up in bed to feed her definitely didn't help with this. Can you imagine any other situation where you'd be expected to do such intensely physical work, using your core strength, when you've just had major surgery? I do not think the effects of C-sections are talked about enough, at any level. We've come a long way, but there's definitely still a way to go.

The week that followed had two different appointments in hospital for Billie, which we could have done in one day, but I thought that was too much for us. In hindsight, I wish we had just got both done at once and didn't have to go through London traffic with a baby who hated the car twice!

We had a few more appointments in hospital for Billie over the next few weeks. During this time, I was still very uncomfortable in general and didn't feel right in my body – I didn't yet feel like me, and I certainly didn't feel like a mum. All these things were happening, like my boobs being huge and swollen, and still having a bump, but the focus was all on the baby. I was too wrapped up in caring for Billie to stop and think about how I was. My mum revealed that she only really felt like a 'mum' when she became more confident taking me out on her own, getting used to it all and feeling less overwhelmed.

Everything is Temporary

The first hospital appointment was to check if Billie had a tongue-tie, because I didn't feel like the latch she had was working for both of us. I never knew bruised nipples were a thing, but that's what I was experiencing, along with little red dots that looked like blood blisters.

At this point, my hormones were still all over the place, so crying every day, multiple times, was my new normal. I cried if Billie fell asleep on me, if she opened her eyes, if she stretched, or if I saw Steve hold her. The list was endless.

I was also crying a lot because of how worried I was about her. What really helped was the antenatal group we were all still a part of. The group had come alive now that most of the babies had been born, mainly with questions like, 'Does your baby get startled and then just go back to sleep?' and 'Is it normal they sound like little warthogs when they sleep?' 'Is it normal that . . .' had become a regular phrase for us all, and I think shows just how unprepared everyone is during this stage of life. Regardless of the books you read, the classes you attend or the advice you get given, until your baby is here, you don't realise half the things you'll need to know. All we're all looking for is a sense of normality, in a new stage of life, where we don't know what normal is anymore. That's why it's such a learning curve, because you're confronted, as an adult, with the knowledge that you don't have all the answers. It's a life stage that is so different to any others – getting married, getting a new job, moving house. What you're doing is something much more permanent – bringing a person into your world.

As it turned out, Billie didn't have a tongue-tie, and the appointment ended up being more about breastfeeding. I was back to square one with this particular issue, and I was disappointed. The midwife went through how I should be holding Billie, and how to take her off my boob by sticking my finger in her mouth. She could tell I had enough supply just by looking at how huge my boobs were, but I felt like such a failure at the time. We had come to see if anything was wrong with Billie, and I left with a sense that I was the one who was doing something wrong. We decided our next step was to get a lactation consultant to visit us at home, and in the meantime we just needed to keep trying. Just as we were walking out of the hospital, my usual midwife Laura was walking in, and, as a shock to no one, I started crying. Again. She asked if I was emotional because I had seen her, and I think that, mixed with all the hormones, got me going even more.

Steve took Billie to change her, and Laura took me into a consultation room that was free, where we went over everything that had been going on, as well as all the questions I had stored in my phone for her. I left feeling so much better. I got to talk to someone I knew and trusted, who was also another mum. Everything I asked her, she told me exactly what I needed to know. I had a cold and Billie had a stuffy nose, so I was convinced I had made her sick and didn't know what to do. Laura recommended saline nose drops and I asked her when to use them. She said that if Billie was struggling to feed, do it then, so she could breathe more easily through her nose. I had the famous snot-sucker, which is a silly and better name for a nasal aspirator, all ready to go in the cupboard, but I was too scared to use it. Now I can look back and realise how fixated I was on every detail. When Billie has a stuffy nose now, I just put the drops up her nose when I remember I have them. Laura also reassured me that I was actually giving Billie antibodies from my cold, and to just keep doing what I was doing. Having a general cold or even a blocked nose with a baby is another level, though. Normally I would stay in bed all day, watch rubbish and have beans on toast, but that was never going to happen again . . .

Our next appointment was for Billie's jaundice. Neither Steve nor I had researched what the tests were like and assumed it would be the same test they did the day after she was born, when they held a tiny device that shone a light on her skin. (We called it the laser beam test.) This was not the case; they needed a blood sample. I thought it would be like the heel-prick test, which was totally fine, but no – the nurse drew her blood from her tiny hand, in the same spot where my cannula had been. It was horrendous for me to watch, but she had a big cry, then fed right after as if nothing happened. I was a total mess, and I could see that Steve looked really upset too. That was in the morning, and by the evening we'd had a call saying all her results were normal. In retrospect, it was a good thing that we didn't look into what would happen, because if I'd known that a needle would be involved, I would have worked myself up. To cheer ourselves up, we decided to have a dirty takeaway at home. When I used to have a horrible day at work, I would treat myself to a steak sandwich and truffle fries from this gorgeous restaurant to end the day on a high. I realised that I had to leave that job when I was ordering it at least once a week and was getting the same guy delivering it each time . . . He must have thought that I had a serious problem.

Once we had got these appointments out of the way, we were open for visitors. I was really worried about having people in the house – and when I say people, I mean family and friends we've known for ages! It wasn't like members of the public were forming a line outside, but we still wanted to do everything we could to protect Billie from the things we could control.

Steve was in charge of all communications, and made a poster of our visitor rules with a flowery background design and emojis for each point!

- No kissing on any part of Billie
- Please wash your hands before cuddles
- To help Mum heal, we're limiting visits to two hours initially
- Only Mum and Dad can feed the baby
- Please don't wear perfume if you want to hold Billie
- No photos of baby's face on social media; check with us before posting anything

The only one I had to fight Steve on was the perfume. My friend had told me that the first time her mother-in-law held her baby, she handed her back smelling of Chanel No 5, and my friend got really upset that she didn't smell like she usually did. It's a very primal thing and Steve just didn't get it at first, but he went along with my wishes.

One day, we had my mum, her brother and his partner round, and, in a two-bedroom basement flat, it was incredibly cramped. This wasn't helped by getting a call from our health visitor, who would be 'popping over' in twenty minutes or so. I'd heard that they didn't schedule when they'd be making home visits so they could see exactly what was going on at home. It was a slight disaster, with all the people in the house, a picky bits lunch everywhere, and me still in my jammies. We spoke about how Billie was, her feeding, how many wet nappies she went through ('a lot' was a sufficient answer), and then finally how I was doing. I'd never met this woman before, so I wasn't super comfortable with telling her how anxious I was. I was saving all of that for my mountain of messages with Laura.

My granny and her sister, my great-aunt Josephine, had health visitors in Glasgow when they gave birth, and they were known as 'green ladies' because of the uniform they wore. Josephine, like my granny, got pregnant and then married very young. There's three years between them and they had five other siblings, but they were always the closest. Josephine left Scotland to teach English in Germany, which is where she met Michael. They had their first son, Marcus, in Glasgow and their second, Anthony, in Cologne. Although she spoke the language, and everyone assumes that with one child already, you don't have time to be lonely, it must have been so hard not being home. I don't think she would have had time to build a new village in a new country, not when she had a toddler to run around after. Granny and Aunt Josephine only had that support for the first five or six months of their children's lives. I'll be able to contact my health visitor until Billie's five and is off to school.

The next milestone during this stage was to get Billie registered. We lived about a ten-minute walk from our local town hall, but at that time, it seemed like another world away. I never knew that you had to get children registered in the town hall in the district where they were born, and because it was Camden, that's where we went. I absolutely loved that her passport would say Camden. So cool – unlike mine, which says High Wycombe (no offence to people who live here, but come on!).

I wanted beautiful pictures of us when we left the house, but it was raining, so we were in raincoats, and so stressed about being on time! When we got there, a woman was screaming and crying at the receptionist about needing to see someone about getting a divorce. It turns out that although town halls handle the legal processes for weddings and civil partnerships, they don't handle separations, which is probably why the woman was so frustrated. Steve and I needed to go together to register Billie because we weren't married. I could have gone on my own, but then Steve's details wouldn't have been on her birth certificate. (Interestingly, when she was first born, her name on her wristbands and the card we were given with her weight had my name on: 'Baby Smith'.)

During this early time in Billie's life, what had started to eat away at me at all these appointments was being asked what kind of birth I'd had. I didn't know that when I decided to have a planned C-section, I would have to justify this decision constantly. I still had a belly, which was now very wobbly, I was still bleeding and wearing my pads and disposable pants, still crying all the time, and had the not-so-small responsibility of getting used to looking after a human being. At the appointment with the health visitor, I just couldn't talk about it anymore. I very calmly said that I had a C-section because it was placenta praevia. I didn't want to go into it any further, so I didn't.

Every time I met anyone in the hospital, we would chat about Billie, and then the last question they would ask was how I was doing. I was under the impression that my worrying was normal – I knew about the hormone drop and about the 'baby blues'. The constant worry about whether your baby is breathing was also something I had heard about – and that doesn't just last for the newborn stage, either! One worry I was not prepared for was waking up and thinking Billie had ended up in the bed somehow. A friend in the antenatal group said this had happened to her, too, and it was such a relief.

Something I knew wasn't normal was how worried I was about Steve. Just over a week after Billie was born, he had a haircut booked and I would be on my own with the baby for the first time, for about thirty minutes. He needed to get out and do something for himself, but I was in a bit of a state. I made him turn his location on on his phone, so I could see exactly where he was, and I made him message me letting me know he had made it there. I had a fear that someone was going to hurt him, either a mugging or a car running him over at a crossing. I couldn't help but think that the worst would happen during this time.

Like all new parents who bring their baby home, as soon as the wee thing falls asleep, I was on constant guard to check if she was still breathing, sometimes even waking her up. I would – and still do – put my hands on Billie's chest to check if it's rising and falling, and put my finger under her nose to feel her hot breath. When I was just weeks old, my mum was contacted by a firm who had newly invented sensor pads that went under a baby mattress that set off a loud beep if the baby stopped breathing for more than twenty seconds. Being anxious parents, and I think just new parents, they decided to buy it, even though I wasn't even in the cot all that much at that time, to be honest. My poor Steve spent hours building Billie's cot months before she was born, just in case she was early, and I don't think she went in it until she was three months old, when I started to get her to nap in it and wanted her to get used to it. On balance, Mum and Dad stopped using the sensor, as they had so many false alarms. It could sometimes go off if I was in a deep sleep, and caused my mum and dad to panic. They must have got such a fright. I know I wouldn't have been able to cope with it. Nowadays, you can get a sock to put on your baby that gives you real-time health readings through an app. It's supposed to make you feel more at peace, but I know I would just be on that app constantly and not just enjoying watching her sleep.

The reason Mum and Dad were so worried was very close to home. In 1991, Anne Diamond, who was TV-am's main presenter before Mum, suffered the unimaginable death of her third child, four-month-old Sebastian, who died from SIDS (sudden infant death syndrome), more usually referred to as cot death. Anne used her pain and suffering to raise awareness of SIDS and spearheaded the 'Back To Sleep' campaign to advise parents to put babies on their backs when you put them in their cot to sleep. Anne had put baby Sebastian on his tummy, which was common practice at the time. Thanks to Anne's tireless campaigning, the number of babies dying of SIDS was reduced significantly. This just shows how accepted customs and practices can change over the years, and that what was once considered the 'right' approach isn't always the case. That's certainly true when it comes to SIDS. Every parent owes Anne Diamond their sincere gratitude. Back in the late 1980s and 90s, Anne was one of the first female presenters to appear on TV while pregnant, and definitely made it easier for Mum to be on GMTV when she was expecting me. It is still very unusual, but Anne paved the way.

It got to three weeks of constant crying for me when I had another appointment with Laura, over the phone. I went through all my questions, including: is it weird that there are feeding cues after she's had a feed? What is a feeding cue? Do I have a velcro baby? She just fed for fourteen minutes with a nappy change in between, is that normal? Does she hate her swaddle suit? She's falling asleep feeding but has a full nappy, but she'll wake up if I change her, so what do I do? My favourite, looking back now, was asking, 'How on earth do you get your baby's hand and footprints for the baby book?!' Something so small like this can feel like such a failure when you try to do it and get back a smudged hand that looks like surrealist art. She told me to wait until Billie was sleeping and use inkless print pads. I had bought a baby nail clipper and a baby electric nail file before Billie was born, and I was horrified when my mum said she just bit my nails off when I was a baby. It turned out that for the first few weeks of Billie's life, her nails were so thin that you could just nibble them off easily . . .

The one thing that really stuck with me after the call was Laura saying that she could hear Billie, who was resting on me, getting upset when I was upset. She said that Billie was clever and could feel how sad I was, which was making her sad. At this time, Billie didn't realise she was separate from me. Babies don't begin to develop a sense of themselves away from their mum until they're around six months old, which is when separation anxiety can kick in for them.

Just as I was slightly calming down and my hormones were returning to some semblance of normal – meaning I was letting Steve leave the house without putting his location on his phone and giving me proof of life every twenty minutes – my worst nightmare came true. The area we lived in North London was a proper community. We had a street WhatsApp group where everyone looked out for one another. People often spoke about seeing a man in the area who had verbally assaulted them, or in some cases had vandalised their cars. We had never seen him before – up until the point we went on one of our first pram walks with Billie. We were crossing the road, with Steve pushing the pram ahead of me as I was walking slower because I was still recovering, when I saw a man close by on his bike. He started swearing at me to hurry up, which I couldn't do anyway, and then he started on Steve, saying he was going to kill him. He stopped in the street, got off his bike and went into more detail about how he was going to 'chop him up in front of his baby'. What makes this even worse was that it happened outside a school, so there were children and other parents around watching it all unfold. This did mean we had witnesses to it, though. Steve clocked that it was the guy we had been warned about multiple times, and decided that the best thing to do was ignore him and keep walking. We got back to the flat, and I was a mess. I called the police, who showed up at our flat quickly and knew exactly who it was we were talking about. Steve used to work as a dispatcher (no, sadly, he never had a uniform) and knew all the lingo the two officers were using. We told the group chat what had happened, and within minutes someone had messaged saying they had seen him. We told the police this, and then they went to arrest him. I suspect that he wasn't a well man, but I felt like he was a risk to my family. I no longer felt safe in my own home. All I wanted to do was scoop up our family and go to my parents' house, but I felt that would be him and my anxiety winning.

I told Laura about this experience and she extended my care, and referred me to the specialist perinatal team to get a GP to prescribe me the same medication I was on before I became pregnant.

This was my initial experience of motherhood, and I really felt like I'd gone through it. I share this not to put anyone off or scare people, but this was what I dealt with. What I know would have helped me in those first few weeks is honesty about what can actually happen. That you may feel extremely anxious, and need help to deal with it. That there will be thoughts and feelings you've never had before swirling around your head. That there are questions you've never had to think of before but now you need the answers to.

MOTHER TO MOTHER

What you have to remember most is that you're not alone – now more than ever. Despite having such a big family, Granny didn't really know her older sisters, Mary and Jacqueline, as they had moved away. Her other older sister, Helen, didn't yet have children, and Josephine and Patzi were younger than Granny, so she had a very small support system. No one had phones then, either; my granny didn't get one until my mum was thirteen and they'd moved to East Kilbride. If your family weren't next door or round the corner, it was hard to keep in touch. As much as I dreaded opening up my social media, not having a phone to quickly look something up, or most importantly keep in touch with my friends with babies, would have made things so much harder.

In the girls-only antenatal group chat, the main consensus was that we had learnt nothing in those initial classes. Some of the mums had sent a very strongly worded email telling the company that runs the course to spend less time on breathwork and more on postpartum. We were all demented! We had no idea how, what or when to put our babies to sleep, if our milk was coming in and how to tell, or if the amount they threw up was normal. That's what we needed from those classes – reassurance, honesty and actual advice. It's my new campaign to tell other mums more about antenatal classes and the things they *don't* tell you. That's why we *have* to use each other!

I had a friend message me saying she was so proud of me becoming a new mum, and that she couldn't tell me how bad it actually is at the beginning. People tend not to tell new parents about those first few weeks, so they are a time of not knowing how to do anything. That's all you can prepare for! My highlights from this time were Billie's first sneezes – she would work herself all up and then sigh like she had done a day's work – and a newborn photo shoot we did at home.

In truth, the first six weeks are about survival. You can't get too caught up in routines and putting any kind of pressure on what you and your baby should be doing. Bouncing back in any way is at the bottom of the agenda. It shouldn't actually be *on* the agenda. A lot of women say that they lose themselves when they become mums. People paint a picture of motherhood as if you're living in a rainbow, forgetting that rain comes first. My life had completely changed but I didn't feel like I had lost *myself*. I had lost my autonomy, yes. I was no longer in control of my decisions, time, appearance and emotions. Being an only child, I'd never known what it was like to not be independent. Spontaneity is out of the window with a baby to look after, and there really is no time for you. If you're not with the baby, feeding them, changing them, getting them to sleep, then you're preparing bottles, cleaning their clothes, or looking at pictures of them on your phone. This is an intense learning phase, and you don't need to be focused on anything other than getting used to a new normal, and living each day with your new baby.

I've focused here on the first few weeks for a reason. Time will pass, and you will learn more – about how to raise a child, but about yourself, too. You will realise you have the greatest capacity for love, and care, and just how much you hate the same three nursery rhymes. In this time, everything is temporary, the good and the bad. You will truly experience the highest of highs and the lowest of lows. You have to be kind, not just to yourself, but to your partner, too.

I have the most beautiful memory of the day Billie got her birth certificate. Steve ordered a birthday cake, to celebrate Billie officially and truly arriving in the world. I have never known anyone to be more obsessed with cake than him, and now he's got another excuse to go all-out.

6

~~Breast is best~~

Fed is Best

When my midwife asked me if I'd thought about breastfeeding, I said I wanted to try, and if it didn't work for whatever reason, I wouldn't beat myself up about it. No one ever said the words 'breast is best' to me, but I knew women who had had this said to them and, culturally, it is an incredibly pervasive way of thinking, even if it is unspoken. My friends that were mums had either exclusively breastfed, combi-fed with formula (like my granny and mum did) after nine months, or used formula from the get-go. The one thing someone did say to me is that there's no medal for breastfeeding your baby, which I appreciated. There's no review at the end where you get a pass or fail on how your baby is fed, so you have to just do what's right for you. It's daunting, but it's your decision, and no one should judge you for it. If they do, they have no idea what they're talking about.

Steve and I had set up our sleep schedule so I could feed Billie every three hours for the first two weeks. We were told to do this by various people to get her back to her birth weight, as it drops when they come out into the world. I had no idea this was a thing, but babies typically lose 5–7 per cent of their birth weight in the first few days after they're born. When Billie was born, she was 8 pounds and 3 ounces, or 3.7 kg, which was a great start, we were told.

I always wanted to give breastfeeding a go, and I remember skipping the chapter on it in the baby books, thinking it's the most natural thing to do, so why would I need to read about it and know about all the different ways you can hold a baby. How naïve I was! The first night we got home, I remember using my electric double pump, because I had used one in the hospital and thought that this was the way to get my milk to come in. I sent a picture to my friend Jo, who I met when I lived in Singapore and had a baby boy just before I left. She had breastfed her son, and her reply was not to go too wild, as boobs work on 'supply and demand'. I had tiny bottles to store milk, so I popped the small amount in the fridge. I just couldn't get my head around the fact that my body was making milk and this is what the baby would drink to stay alive.

I was fixated on getting my supply up and, looking back now, it wasn't healthy. I obviously wanted Billie's birth weight to increase and for her to be healthy, but I put a huge amount of pressure on myself to get the milk going. The first six weeks of breastfeeding establish your supply, and I was convinced that if I missed the three-hour mark of feeding her, it would just disappear. I used to wake Billie up with kisses to feed her, to make it more fun, which was glorious. With hindsight, I wouldn't do this again, as she was feeding well anyway, was at a healthy weight and was gaining her

Fed is Best

weight back. I wish I had stuck to feeding her when she wanted it, because I didn't have to worry about her weight. She was a good size when she was born and loved her milk. In our sleep schedule, I could have slept a bit longer, but this was at the very beginning, when she didn't sleep unless she was on someone. I had my iPad set up and a million snacks. By the time I got her to sleep in her cot next to our bed, I had watched all eleven seasons of *Vanderpump Rules*. (It had always been on my list, and it really surpassed my expectations. Reality TV before social media and before proper hair and make-up is a time that should never be forgotten about.)

I did manage to do something productive in that time, which was order birth-announcement cards and then write people letters saying thank you for their gifts. All one-handed, while Billie was sleeping soundly on my chest.

The shifts of sleep Steve and I had agreed on weren't working for me anymore. I really missed my mornings, because the day for me started when I woke up from my break at 11 a.m. I had missed watching Mum's show, and having any kind of breakfast, and I really wanted a bit more of a routine.

After those feeds every three hours, I messaged Laura to ask: what now? I thought maybe now there would be a feed every four hours, and that it would move up hour by hour until Billie was on solids. I had no idea! Laura said to just feed Billie whenever she wanted food. This sounds so simple, but it filled me with dread. I had no idea when Billie was hungry.

Jo was always on the other end of the phone for advice. She sent me a list of the different cries babies have:

MOTHER TO MOTHER

- Neh – Hungry cry
- Owh – Sleepy cry
- Heh – Discomfort cry
- Eair – Gas cry
- Eh – Burp cry

All the crying sounded the same to me! I didn't know what Billie wanted, which made me feel like such a failure, because all the sayings go, '*You* know your baby best', 'Trust *your* gut.' I had no clue what was normal or what she needed, but I felt like I was supposed to know. This all came to a head when, after one feed, Billie just wouldn't burp for me. I asked Steve to help and she did it immediately, so, naturally, I cried for a solid half-hour, saying that I just couldn't do anything right.

He didn't really know what to say and, to be honest, there was nothing he could have done or said that would have made me feel better. It was clearly all in my head, but when you're in it, you're in it. One night, I couldn't get to sleep when it was my turn. This was quite normal for me. It was due to a mix of not being able to switch off and not having Billie either in my belly anymore, or on my chest. She was away in the living room with Steve, and it might as well have been a different country. The white-noise machine was cranked up, I had my eye mask on, and I had lathered my chest with magnesium lotion to try to help me nod off. It usually took me an hour to get to sleep, but when Steve came in to take over, I realised I hadn't actually slept at all.

I switched my normal viewing of *Vanderpump Rules* to *Below Deck Mediterranean*. This was one of the mums from the antenatal classes' midnight feeding watch, and we were exchanging messages at 3 a.m. about our dream boat charter. Which captain we'd want – Captain Lee (obviously) – which chef – again, the obvious choice of OG chef Ben – our deckhands and stews – which would have to be led by Kate, as well as our charter from hell – we both agreed that the boat with the gold swan taps would make us want to return to land.

It was soon time to switch over, and when Steve took Billie, this time I actually slept. This was the start of the issue. (Before I get into it, Steve didn't actually do anything wrong, but at the time, it would be safe to say that I wanted to kill him.) I woke up hours later, because he had let me sleep. This meant that I didn't then get to feed Billie on the three-hour mark, and in my head that meant that my milk would dry up and she would never be able to feed from me ever again. What made the situation worse was that he had chosen to give her formula.

We took pre-made mini formula bottles with us to the hospital, a pack of six 70ml bottles. She got through it in two days, and the midwives gave her more that they had in stock. I was worried because it was a different brand, but as long as it's the same type, like either cow's milk or soy, it's fine. The first night when we got home and I was calling Laura about how to use our pump, when to feed her and just generally what to do, she said that I needed to make a decision on feeding and stick to it. Out of the options she told me, which were exclusively breastfeeding, combi feeding or moving just to formula, I decided to give just breastfeeding a go. The issue for me after that was, I had it in my head that if she got formula at any point, she would reject feeding from me, and then reject me.

The morning of her birth, I remember calling my best friend, crying and saying, 'What if she gets here and doesn't like me?' I think I then consciously paired this feeling with feeding, as it was all I could really do with her at this point. My thought process was, if I can't make milk or Billie won't take it, what's the point of me being her mum, as surely anyone else could look after her. This was a very unhealthy thought that also signalled to me that I needed to go back on anxiety medication. Instead of snapping at Steve, which I had done in my sleep-deprived state, I decided to write down in my phone why I was so angry and upset with him for choosing formula to feed her. I also sent him links from the NHS website about the importance of keeping up my supply, and it's fair to say that the message was received: if Billie was hungry, which was all the time, he had to come and wake me up. I didn't need to beat myself up, though, over one feed being not what I wanted.

After one of our hospital visits, we booked an appointment with a lactation consultant to come to the house through the Breastfeeding Network. Someone from the team had come to see us when we were in hospital to give us a leaflet and have a chat, but I very naïvely didn't think we'd need them. How hard could the most natural thing – feeding your baby – be? Well, as it turns out, very. Billie had a really good latch on one side, but the other side was just not happening.

I was so lucky that Jane, the lactation consultant, visited us at home. She brought a crochet boob and a doll to show me the best positions for feeding, and then got me feeding Billie on each boob in front of her to nail the latch. She was able to spot that Billie had a white lump on the roof of her mouth, which was a blister from not being able to latch on right. When I heard the word 'blister', I started crying, but Jane said it was totally normal. At this stage with my hormones, once I'd started crying, I couldn't stop for a while. I think normally Jane would stay for half an hour or so, but that day she stayed with me for hours. We ended up talking about our births – she'd had her boys in the same hospital I had Billie – and how mental it is to be surviving on a couple of hours sleep. The most important thing she said was to remember that you and your baby are a team. It's not just you who is doing a whole lot of learning; your baby also needs to learn how this whole thing works.

What eventually did give me a bit of rest was storing milk. I would leak from the boob Billie wasn't feeding on, and angel midwife Laura told me to get a 'milk collector' after I'd sent her some messages on what to do. My mum's midwife, Precious, stayed on after her shift to see me into the world. The level of care was different then, so it wasn't the same person she saw for appointments or scans, but she still remembers how kind she was, even well after thirty years. She never got to see Precious again in any postnatal care, but she did get sent a present of a rose ornament from her, because of my name.

I ordered a manual breast pump that looked like a mini water bottle that attached to your nipple. (The amount of Amazon deliveries I got during this time was mental. I think new parents funded the Bezos wedding in Venice). I would get anywhere from 30ml to 80ml, so it was quite inconsistent. The worrying about pumping was almost paralysing for me, as I was told to not miss a feed so I could pump, but then how would Billie eat if I missed a feed to pump? She was always going to be either near me or on me, so I didn't really need to pump, but having a bit stored meant Steve could feed her so I could have a nap or spoil myself with a shower, but also have time to bond with her.

However, my days with the handy pump were numbered. Billie discovered the joy of kicking, and I ended up with milk all over me. The phrase 'Don't cry over spilt milk' clearly doesn't mean breast milk you've spent a long time expressing. In the end, I settled on a hands-free breast pump that looked like a boob, which I could pop in my bra and not worry about it being knocked off. I would then pop the milk into little storage bags, labelling them with the date, the time of day and the amount.

In today's world, social media is a constant background noise to everyone's lives. My social media algorithms had obviously shown me nothing but motherhood content for ages. At this time, I was seeing so many things about feeding on Instagram. How, if your baby has milk you expressed or pumped in the morning at night, they'll then think it's morning and be awake for hours. The algorithm clearly knew I was struggling with feeding, and everything that was coming up was trying to hook me in and keep me scrolling for hours. I was already exhausted, and I didn't need people online giving me their 'advice' or trying to sell me things. I had Laura for advice, and my own Amazon

Fed is Best

spending habits for that! I'd be shown a video of a woman showing off how much milk she had pumped, and the caption would be along the lines of: 'I have the secret to upping your supply, comment "milk" and I'll DM you', or 'Worried about how much your baby is getting from you? Subscribe to my newsletter.' I honestly think things like this are unhelpful and even potentially harmful. That might be a tad harsh, but when it's three in the morning, you're sleep-deprived and everything hurts, you want someone to tell you everything's going to be OK, not prey on your fears or try to get money from you. It's a vulnerable time for anyone, and this is why when any mum-to-be asks me anything now, I tell them absolutely everything, give them my number and tell them to call me at any time for a chat or some support. The best thing I did was limit my screen time on social media and start charging my phone in the kitchen rather than by my bed. Steve bought me one of those alarm clocks that lights up like a sunrise. I already had an alarm clock – we had made a human one – but having this to tell the time was great.

These first few weeks, I really realised that all the gadgets and stuff you think you need aren't that important. Your bed becomes like an island, and by my bedside table had my nappy caddy with all the bits I could refill. It had nappies, wipes, nappy bags, muslins, nappy cream, lavender pillow spray to get me to relax, moisturiser for me, a spare bodysuit and puppy pads for spillage, and snacks. Chocolates like Celebrations or Heroes were fab because it was always a surprise what I'd get. Another must-have was a face mist that I'd use to wake me up for a feed. My mum's stylist,

Bronaugh, had two tiny babies, and she told me to drink sugar-free Red Bull for the long nights. Genius.

I messaged Jo and Charlie to say that they were being kind when they didn't tell me I'd completely lost the plot when I asked them if I should get a wet-wipe warmer that cost fifty quid. In my head, I thought it would be a shock for her wee bum being cleaned with a cold cloth, but I think people have managed without one . . . Especially my mum and granny. My mum confessed she bought me far too many clothes for when I was just born, something I did for Billie too, but in a less practical way. I did wear the clothes my mum had for me, but the 0–3 months dress I got Billie never made it out of the wardrobe. We were thick in double-zipped sleepsuits, and that was about it.

The night before we went to get Billie registered with the GP, I wanted to get her to sleep in her cot. I can tell you, it was a night of hell. I downloaded an app that tracked everything she did: sleeping; if she'd done a poo or a wee; feeding (it even let me know how long she had been on each boob). I shoved Steve in the spare room, as I just wanted to see if I could do it. Every time I would put her down, she would cry. I'd then do a pretty relentless ritual of changing her, feeding her, burping her (so she wouldn't then be sick lying down when I'd change her), and cuddling her to sleep. Steve came in in the morning around seven and said he would take over so I could get a shower. I know this was supposed to be my 'me time', but I was convinced she was crying. It turned out to be 'phantom cries', and not washing the shampoo out of my hair was something I needed to get used to for a while until this stopped.

It was a ten-minute walk to the GP, which is exactly how much sleep I got the night before. I was a zombie, but we made it. I managed to fill her registration form in on only the second attempt (I got the year wrong for her date of birth on the first attempt) and then made it back home. Steve said I should have come and got him to take over for a bit, but I wanted him to have a break and to get her used to not being on someone to sleep. This whole episode made me realise that just because I *can* do something on my own, it doesn't mean I *have* to.

That night was a lot, but it was worth it. Billie had finally got the gist of sleeping independently. I messaged my mum the next few nights with updates on how long she was managing, messages relaying that she had had a solid two hours as if it was the most groundbreaking news.

Something I didn't know about feeding was how it feels like the energy is being sucked out of you. Someone told me that breastfeeding a baby is equivalent to walking seven miles each day, and I wish I'd known that earlier on. I would get so worked up about not doing anything all day apart from feeding Billie, changing her and getting her to sleep, and apart from the lack of sleep, I couldn't understand why I was so shattered. My mum explained the exhaustion to me as jet lag, but worse. She said she'd had it a lot easier because when she went back to work, she was up at 3 a.m. anyway to start the day.

I often felt like I was failing with feeding, even after finding a bit of equilibrium with it. We went through the joys of cluster feeding and, at the time, I messaged my friend Rhiannon, from the antenatal classes, to ask if it was normal for babies to constantly be on them. Cluster feeding was described to me as needing to do a feed every twenty minutes, but I was sitting in the rocking chair with Billie for five hours without moving. I did selfishly love feeding her when we had guests round, because I could sneak away and have some time, just us two. No one else could hold her and I was totally in control.

Rhiannon told me about a breastfeeding clinic she went to a few times and said it really helped, so I made the huge decision to leave the house by myself. I was filled with dread. The anxiety of being on my own hit me; how would I get there, how would I feed her on the go, how did I work the car seat? I couldn't lift her into the pram or seat because I was still recovering from the C-section. I couldn't walk there as it was too far away, so I decided to treat myself for the big day and get a cab.

I had a pram that folded up and turned into a car seat, a fabulous gadget my parents both couldn't get over. The thing that blew their minds the most was our car seat that swivelled around so we could face Billie when putting her in. Tiny things like this were making our lives so much easier than they had been for our parents a few decades ago.

Rhiannon was there for support too, and it was the first time I had seen her without a bump and with a baby. She was a week behind me and was having a bit of a tough time with an undiagnosed tongue-tie that had been found about a month in. Someone else came into the room and went to sit down next to one of the volunteers. I gathered she'd been there before, and I overheard her say something along the lines of 'It's got a lot better.' She then very casually took her boob out, and her entire nipple was gone. The areola was there, but the actual nipple tip had disappeared. Could that happen?! She left first and I caught up on all things feeding. I asked what was going on with the amount of milk I was able to get from the boob Billie wasn't feeding from. One day, it would be 60ml, the next day, at the same time, just 10ml. They told me not get too worried and try to rest. I could always be woken up by Steve if there was not enough milk when I was sleeping, and it was also good practice for Billie to have a bottle. Another thing that put me at ease was that one of the women who volunteered took one look at Billie and said she was 'well fed'.

Going out on my own for the first time not only gave me the confidence that everything was actually OK, but also showed me that there were people out there ready to give support if I needed it. I think this is probably something that was available to my mum and granny, but in a different way. I had access to medical professionals when I needed them, whereas Mum and Granny relied on the people around them much more. The family and friends who had already had children – especially for my granny.

Billie was going to make her debut on Mum's show later that week, and now I felt much more confident at the prospect of taking Billie to an actual TV set! My mum was desperate to show her off to the world, and I thought it was such a beautiful thing to do because she had done it with me when I was born. This was the first time I didn't even try on what I was going to wear to go on TV. I just wasn't important enough anymore. I packed four outfits for Billie with matching bibs, and even muslins that would complement the colours in her babygros.

I was a bit worried about people maybe commenting on some dry skin she had on her face. It went along her eyebrows like a monobrow of rough, bumpy spots. She had scratched one of them off in her sleep, so it had scabbed over, leaving a noticeable mark just above her left eye. The antenatal mum WhatsApp group was on fire, and we were all sharing pictures of our babies' poos, sick and skin, asking each other if it was normal. I had already sent a picture of a tiny white spot that Billie had on her cheek to Laura, who said to dab some breastmilk on it. It worked wonders, so when a picture of something similar came up on the group, it was my time to shine with the advice. I couldn't believe that I was the one helping someone with a baby.

We had to leave around half five in the morning, and there was a 50/50 chance Billie would be up. Of course when she actually had to be up at this time, she was soundly asleep. I woke up an hour before we were supposed to leave to get myself ready and then sort her out. I stayed at my mum's the night before, so she was on hand. She normally has a shower, gets into comfies, ties her hair up still wet and jumps in the car to get glam at work. Helen, who's been my mum's hair and make-up artist for nearly three decades, made me look like a human being, and I got my jumpsuit on. I forgot about the shoes, so I was in my tattered trainers, thinking no one would be looking at my feet. I look back at the pictures now . . .

I changed Billie before we went on because I was so worried about her leaking through on the telly. I should have just let her sleep, but I wouldn't be told! At that point, whenever we had to leave the house, we would always change her, feed her, burp her, and then very likely need to change her again. (Nothing can prepare you for the amount of poo a newborn can do.) This then meant that, because she was awake, she was hungry. I didn't want to whip my boob out on national television, so I had a bottle of expressed milk ready from that morning. I was going on with Dr Hilary, and it was just like it was when my mum took me on GMTV when I was a few weeks old. If you look at that footage, you can see my mum giving me water from a beaker, which now is a complete no-no. (The advice now is that fully breastfed babies don't need water until they're six months old.) In 1994, my mum was sitting next to Dr Hilary doing this and no one batted an eyelid. She breastfed me for nine months, so I would have been having milk then too. It was the same with my granny. She gave my mum and her brother Graham water, plus cod liver oil and orange juice. Not giving babies water is one of those things that 'they' say. The 'famous they' was something my granny and great-aunt Josephine would say to each other, and then roll their eyes simultaneously. Rhiannon told me that when her aunt was born, she was given water at night for the first seven nights, so that by the time her parents took her home, she didn't need a feed in the middle of the night. Their nights were maybe six or seven hours, right from the start. This advice was published in 1948, when mums would normally be in the hospital for ten days after giving birth. I'm not sure when this advice stopped.

Billie kicked off on my mum's show big time. The six minutes of being on the sofa felt like a good, solid hour. The chat started with just how beautiful she was (obviously), and then Dr Hilary asked how I was doing. Billie decided to start crying, and my mum picked her up and started rocking her, while I told Hilary about how anxious I'd been.

I felt like I was over the worst of the anxiety at this point. I remember one night there was a storm, and of course I was awake, and I was convinced someone had a torch and was trying to come into the house. In my head, someone was going to come in, harm us and then leave. I didn't feel weird talking about these really personal topics with Dr Hilary, because I'd grown up with him and the setting we were in. I used to come to work with Mum to see bands on GMTV, then I read the news for the rehearsals for *Daybreak*, and there was also the famous Westlife incident (I wouldn't let go of Brian McFadden. I was quite literally clinging to his neck during a reunion with the boys' families, who they hadn't seen for months. I was obsessed and was also only six.)

Once we came off the show, Billie promptly fell asleep on the walk back to Mum's dressing room. No one said anything about her skin, not even Dr Hilary. Even though I had sick on me and Mum had to grab her to calm her down on national TV, she was perfect. I messaged Dr Amir, who is also a resident doctor on Mum's show, on the way home and he rang me immediately. He said it was cradle cap, and it was going to get crusty, then go back to baby-soft, beautiful skin. Weirdly, Billie then got it on her actual 'cap' and

Fed is Best

the best thing I did was buy this very special sponge and brush to use in the shower that scraped it all away. There was a real temptation to pick it all off, but scraping it gently away with that brush was one of the most satisfying things I've ever done.

7

~~'Mine slept through the night by then'~~
Every Baby is Different

No baby is the same and sleep is the thing that made me fully realise this. I could count on Billie napping – it took her a while, but when she was down, she was down. I had friends whose wee ones napped a few times in the day for just ten minutes, and heard a horror story from one mum of her son only sleeping for forty minutes one night. Steve's mum would regularly say that he slept through the night by nine weeks. My mum said that I didn't sleep through until I was fourteen months!

The week that followed going on the show was my hardest one yet. Just as I'd been on TV talking about getting over the worst of my anxiety, my body decided to take that as a signal for its time to shine. In the first few weeks of Billie's life, as I was breastfeeding, I had noticed some small lumps in my armpit and, after chatting to the WhatsApp mum group, I learnt that a few others had it and had managed to massage them away. I wasn't engorged and was producing milk, so I wasn't worried, and they would come and go. It wasn't until a week after messaging the group that I noticed a small lump on the left side of my left boob. I didn't think anything of it. I had my best friend Ruby over for a walk, with another friend I had met at university, and who was one of the first people I told I was pregnant when I went to Orkney on Mum's book tour. The last time I had been to Orkney was to see her and celebrate New Year's there, and we went to the island's one nightclub, Fusion, had a pitcher of bright-green liquid and danced on the carpeted dance floor. This time, we had slices of cake the size of my head in Sheila Fleet – a café and jewellery shop. A very different vibe.

We walked together into Islington to look at the shops, and it took me a good ten minutes to realise I had two other adults with me – so why was I pushing the pram? Then the lump on my boob started to hurt because my arm was rubbing against it as I walked. I went to the loo when we stopped at a café, and when I inspected my boob, the whole area was now red. It was Sunday evening and we had Billie's vaccines and my check-up a few days later, so I thought that I'd just see the doctor then. I was trying to be present and chat to Ruby, who I never get to see, when I started to feel really faint. I got home without saying anything, and then once they'd both left I asked Steve to have a look. It was now a massive lump and bright red, so I decided to call 111. It was 7 p.m., and for all the faults and issues people talk about with the NHS, the help I got was incredible. I was told it was probably mastitis, that I needed to get antibiotics as soon as possible, and that I needed to keep feeding through it. I got an appointment with a doctor at 9 p.m. about a twenty-minute drive away. Being in a taxi by myself was bizarre. Being anywhere by myself at this point was bizarre! Steve stayed at home with Billie and I fed her before I left, thinking that she would then be OK.

The day before the lump arrived, I had had a four-hour break from expressing or feeding. Billie had a bottle of expressed milk from Steve, so she wasn't hungry, but it was the longest I'd ever gone without feeding her. I have no idea if a milk duct got blocked because of that, which led to the mastitis, or if it was an infection. But it was getting worse by the minute at this point, and I felt awful. I felt so cold and was almost shivering, but I was also sweating. If I'd waited until Tuesday to see the doctor, God knows what state I would have been in. It's not that I wouldn't put myself first, I just literally wasn't able to anymore. For anything else that was that wrong with me, I would have called sooner and not let it get as bad if I didn't have Billie.

My appointment was at a normal GP's office but at night, so all the main lights were off and no one was there. Very zombie apocalypse. The doctor had to ask the female receptionist to be a chaperone before I got my boob out to confirm it was mastitis. I thought I'd have to then get another taxi to a late-night pharmacy for the antibiotics but he had them there in a cupboard for such occasions. He told me I needed to keep feeding from that boob and to rest. Whenever anyone told me to rest, I would just look at them plainly. I didn't have copious amounts of free time to 'rest'.

I got back around 10 p.m., and Steve said Billie hadn't stopped crying. It wasn't a hungry cry, it was a guttural cry of sheer unhappiness. He had tried everything, and nothing had worked. As soon as I fed her, she was fine. I could see how upset he was about not being able to soothe her. He said that she just wanted me and didn't even like him. It was important to me to keep telling him that, biologically, Billie would be more attached to me when she was this tiny. It's not something he or even Billie could control.

That night was rough. I had started taking the antibiotics and was on paracetamol, but the best thing would have been ibuprofen to reduce the swelling (which I wasn't allowed to take anymore because I'd had an asthma flare-up after the birth). Steve was back at work and, as much as I missed him constantly being available and sharing the mental load of everything, I did feel like it was time to get into a routine and get used to our new normal. The six weeks of leave he got was enough for us. Some of the partners of mums on our WhatsApp group were back at work after two weeks, which to me is just wild.

I rang my mum and asked if she could come round the next morning. It was a very happy coincidence that it was the October half-term and she wasn't working, so as soon as she could, she was on the train to ours. She came in, scooped Billie up and let me sleep for the whole day with wake-ups to feed her. It got to about 5 p.m. when I asked if she could stay. Steve was sleeping on the sofa bed in his office that was also the nursery, and I didn't want Mum on the living room sofa, so she decided that it would be best to be in with me, because that way she could help lift Billie on to me.

My mum had the full experience of Billie that night. I think it was around 4 a.m. and Billie's third wake-up when I was mid-changing her, and she did the biggest wee that went through to the duvet and bedsheets. We'd just bought a mattress protector a few weeks before, thank God. I helped Mum strip the bed, but because it was dark and I wanted to keep it dark for Billie, Mum ended up putting the new mattress protector on inside out, and we just gave up on a new cover for the duvet. While I was feeding Billie, my mum got to see how I expressed milk from the other boob, and we had our first 'we didn't have that in my day' conversation. She said that when she fed me, her other boob would just leak through her clothes. Mum said that she didn't remember it being this hard. Whenever I asked her if I was like this, or what to do with a nappy rash, she couldn't answer. Your brain must hardwire to forget so you want to have more children . . .

This was the point for me when I realised how important help is. I needed my mum and felt so sorry for people who didn't have theirs in their lives. There was a lot of crying after that thought. If I had stayed in Singapore and had a baby there, who would have helped me? If my mum was living halfway across the world, she couldn't have come in a matter of hours to wash my hair after the birth or help get the sticky patches of my plasters from my scar off. I know I had Steve, but it's different when you're at your lowest. You just need your mum.

I was able to leave the house for Billie's vaccine appointment and my check-up a few days later. I thought with having had a C-section, the doctor would have looked at my scar, but this was a chat about my mental health, then about contraception. That was it. He spoke about getting the coil, and I just looked at him and said I would be using the method of abstinence. I looked like I was around five months pregnant but with a very squishy belly at this point, I had new stretchmarks on my boobs from feeding, and I was the hairiest I've ever been. I also had this massive scar I still hadn't looked at. The only person seeing me naked for the foreseeable would be Billie. Poor thing.

We then waited to see the nurse for Billie's first round of vaccines. I was dreading this. People had given me the tip of feeding her while it happened. The nurse was so lovely, which helped, and she said that it would be over quickly for Billie and I'd be the one more upset, which is exactly what happened. The first vaccination was for Rotavirus, and gave us all a false hope for how the rest would go down. It was a liquid in a tiny sachet that was just squirted into her mouth, and she absolutely loved it. She was then given an injection in each thigh. We had dressed her in a sleepsuit with zips for easy access. The first injection was the 6-in-1 vaccine for horrible illnesses like diphtheria, hepatitis B, HiB, polio, tetanus and whooping cough. The second one was for MenB, which can cause meningitis, septicaemia and sepsis. I fed her before each injection and she cried, went bright red, and then went right back to feeding. She was fine, but I was an absolute state.

We stupidly took her in the carrier, because the walk to the doctor's was only ten minutes, but because the injections were in her thighs, I didn't want to strap her back in, so Steve carried her home. He was singing away to her, she was very happy and I was still crying. After another feed, she was shattered and had a really long nap. I think having that appointment later in the day was such a good idea, so we could just go home, get into bed and be comfy.

After a few days, my flu-like symptoms had stopped, but my boob was so sore, red and hot, and the lump hadn't gotten much smaller. I decided to do the old wives' tale of freezing cabbage and popping one of the leaves on my boob. The shape of the leaves are perfect to cup a boob. While it was very cooling to start, I realised almost immediately that I had made a big mistake. No one had said anything about using a paper towel or tea towel to separate your skin from the leaf. Essentially what had happened was the heat from my boob cooked the cabbage, and our whole flat started to smell awful.

There were multiple times I thought about packing in breastfeeding because of this. But I worried a lot about how I would cope with the logistics of formula, the bottles needing to be constantly washed and sterilised, how much I would need to make, judging when it would be cool or warm enough for her. We were really lucky with Billie that she loved her milk and would have any of it that was expressed cold, right out of the fridge. I think she would have sucked the milk out of a deodorant stick. This, though, then brought worry that she wasn't getting enough from me. Either way I looked at it, I felt this huge anxiety. I kept going with breastfeeding, and just as the lump had started to disappear, I noticed a rash on the same side, near my bra strap. I'd had shingles before, so knew this was what it was. I sent a voice note to the group chat I had with Charlie and Jo moaning about how, just as I was getting better, everything was going wrong again. Jo said something that stuck with me: that 'One day you will get your body back, but right now it's not yours.'

Women's bodies are constantly spoken of throughout their lives, and especially the changes we go through during pregnancy and birth. I don't think women's bodies are celebrated enough after giving birth. You've grown the baby, given birth to the baby and now have to feed the baby. It would have been nice for the dad to maybe take one of the three here!

I was just coming off the antibiotics for mastitis, and now I was back on medication for shingles. Added to the mix, Billie started touching the mastitis as she fed from that side, so I had to use massive plasters to cover it. I then had a reaction to the plasters, which created a lovely square border of blisters. I couldn't make it up! My back was also in pieces from feeding her, and I eventually did something for myself and used heat patches – when I remembered I had them.

My mum told me she was speaking to women at work about my experiences, telling them that I had mastitis and that she had spent her week off basically being a carer to me. She said someone very casually said they had been hospitalised because of it; another said she had had it and had to stop breastfeeding. I remember thinking, 'Hang on, sorry, this woman was in hospital? How is that OK?' I think because having a baby is seen as what women 'do', all the things that go along with it are taken for granted. It's a big deal and it should be treated that way. I feel like conversations now, had by millennials and Gen X generations, are the most honest and open when really talking about motherhood. For my granny and my mum, there wasn't as much noise as there is now – but we're also telling it like it is. There is still so much further to go in terms of acknowledging all the realities of life as a new mother, but speaking out and sharing our experiences really does help to demystify motherhood.

As I was getting over everything, I had our first family trip away to Scotland and Billie's first flight to prepare for up. We decided to stay in one of our potential wedding venues to scope it out, so we went to Cromlix near Dunblane. We knew instantly that we wanted to get married there. It was so beautiful, and such a great place to show off Scotland to all our friends and family who had never been.

The trip couldn't have come at a better time, as I really needed a change of scenery. Our flat and in particular our bedroom had become a place that I just didn't want to be in anymore. I associated it with either Billie or me crying, no sleep, and just feeling like rubbish.

We cheated a bit with the packing for this trip. My parents were driving up, and we were flying. Steve and I just took hand luggage, and naturally filled Mum and Dad's entire boot and back seat up with our stuff. I made them take a bath, a travel cot, two suitcases filled with clothes and nappies, a play gym and toys Billie had never used, or would use for months. We didn't even use the bath in the end; we just shoved her bum in the sink when there was a poo explosion! The hotel also got us a cot too, with a blanket for her.

Our biggest worry was Billie being unsettled. Whenever she cried, I just put her on one of my boobs, so I had started a campaign with Steve to use a dummy. I had one when I was wee, but neither Steve nor his siblings ever did. He was very unsure, but we had made it to eight weeks without one and I wanted to give it a go, just to see if it would make her stop crying for a bit and bring a bit of comfort. At this point, Billie hated the car. I tried toys, making silly faces, singing, but nothing worked until we got to wherever we were going and I had either picked her up for a cuddle or fed her. It's no wonder she was described as 'well fed'!

We had just made it out of the driveway when she started crying. I took the executive decision to try the dummy, and immediately she stopped crying and started sucking. It was very strange for a few minutes because of how quiet it was, but then we started enjoying it. She was happier! For the rest of the journey to Heathrow, Steve ordered a bunch of dummies, dummy clips and a little box to keep a spare dummy in that you can attach to a bag or the pram. I had followed an instinct and it had paid off. This was a huge win, and it made me realise I needed to not only listen to myself more, but trust myself, too.

We didn't need to *play* dumb once we got the airport, as we genuinely had no idea what we were doing with a baby in tow. We folded up the car seat/pram and didn't know if we needed to leave it at the gate, the plane door or even take it on the plane with us. We asked the woman at the gate and she took pity on us, letting us board then and telling us to leave it at the plane door. Steve had booked us right at the back of the plane, so it was easy to get on and off and get to the loo if we needed to change her. It turned out that the very short flight of just over an hour meant

My mum and granny in Glasgow Green. They used to go to Richmond Park and the Cathkin Braes for picnics and to feed the ducks. Granny was always so smartly dressed. She was just twenty-one years old here.

April 1962

September 1972

My mum's granny (my great-granny Kelly) and my mum at her flat, the multistorey in Dalmarnock, in Glasgow. Mum was so proud of these bright red shiny boots that laced up, and her trendy midi dress – very fashionable back then. This was her 'outfit for best' and was worn over and over again until she grew too big for it.

My granny, my mum and Uncle Graham outside Woolies in Glasgow. These stores were once a high street institution and just about every kid would sneak a sweetie from the pick and mix. Mum was not pleased when Graham came along as she was no longer the spoiled only child.

September 1967

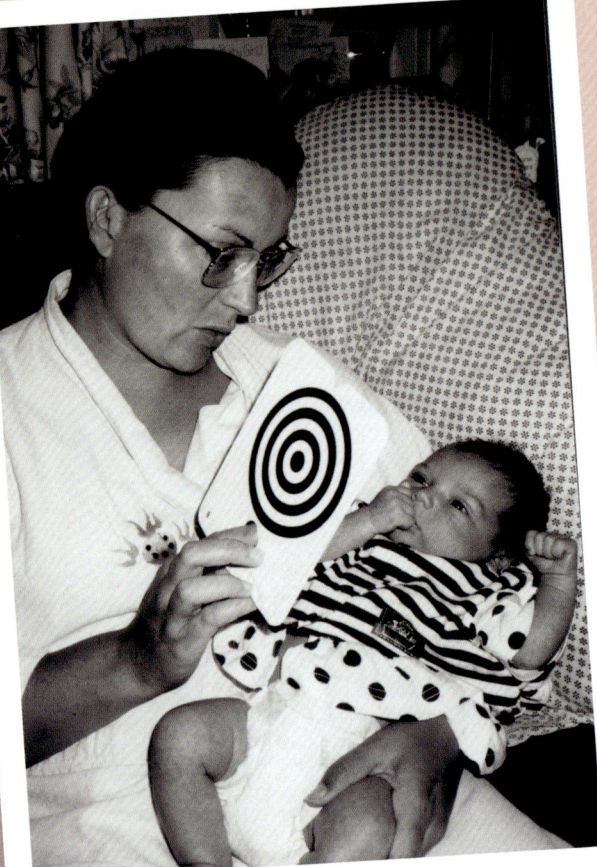

I was a real water baby and would play in the pool for hours. On this holiday in Spain, we re-enacted *The Little Mermaid* every day. Mum was Ursula.

June 1998

I was a few weeks old here. Mum bought these black and white cards which had just come out to help stimulate newborn babies. I had them dangling over my cot and in front of my face a lot.

June 1994

First proper pic of Billie with her eyes open!

September 2024

Mum and Dad took me all over the world. This was us in Florida. I would stay awake during most long-haul flights and only fall asleep when the plane was about to land . . . frazzled parents and angelic baby. I have no idea how they did it.

August 1996

Me and Mum in Shapinsay, Orkney, where I took my first steps.

July 1995

August 1994

July 1999

My granny came down to help a lot when I was tiny. She would play with me for hours and rock me to sleep singing Scottish nursery rhymes. We'd do a lot of dressing up and being silly, which is exactly what my mum is like with Billie.

My granny on holiday in Majorca, Spain, aged thirty-eight. She was channelling Joan Collins and had matching black polka dot sandals. Fabulous.

August 1979

December 1994

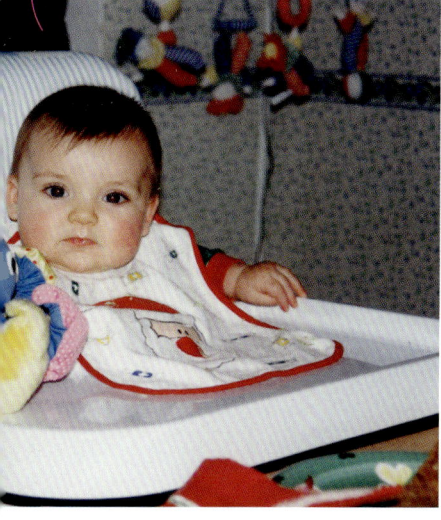

Me in my happy place: in my highchair, waiting for food.

This is the picture where I think I look the most like Billie. Mum always managed to get tartan in somewhere.

March 1995

August 2025

Billie in the pool in Spain with her granny and grandad (while I finished writing this book inside) and loving her first time on a swing.

June 2025

May 1995

July 1995

Me and my dad. He made me laugh a lot when I was a baby, and still does. Dad had an MG red sports car that he restored, but he never drove it after I was born. It sat outside the house and was a giant toy for me.

Billie waking up next to her daddy. If someone starts yawning, the other person can't help it.

November 2024

First lunch with Granny and Grandad, after moving out of London to live ten minutes away from them.

June 2025

September 2025

Billie fitting right in at her granny's studios, cheering Steve on during his Ultra Marathon and celebrating her first birthday with a party animal themed party.

September 2025

August 2025

Four generations at my great-granny Kelly's house in Glasgow for a Christmas visit. Mum has put me in a very festive tartan dress.

December 1997

Billie meets her very own great-granny Kelly on my first Mother's Day.

March 2025

that she slept the whole way! The abundance of stuff we'd brought with us never made it out of the bag. I'd built up this outing in my head so much, and then the next thing I knew, we were just *doing it* and it was actually fine.

The next thing I needed to think about was how on earth we were going to sterilise her bottles (and now dummies) in the hotel. For the first time, I had asked for help on social media. Up to this point I had avoided it because I was so worried about being trolled. The flurry of supportive messages was such a relief. People told me to ask the hotel for a microwave and get steriliser bags, as well as the sterilising tablets you could use with cold water. I went with the tablets, and I washed everything in the sink with warm soapy water (I took a travel bottle of fairy liquid with me), and then filled the sink with cold water, added the tablet and left everything to sterilise for fifteen minutes.

I'm so glad we did this trip when she was so tiny. In my head, as soon as we had a baby, we would never go out for dinner or go to a hotel again. With her being less than three months old, her schedule was all over the place, and we were able to take her in the pram to the restaurant because she just slept. Having her in the restaurant in her pram wouldn't last, as we'd soon be in a routine of her having to go to bed, so we fully embraced the holiday mode of all the rules going out the window. I got dressed up and everything. I had to buy new clothes because I was officially a size up, and I couldn't be in my normal uniform of an oversized jumper and leggings that were usually covered in sick. Shopping for those clothes wasn't a great experience. I didn't want to try anything on in the shop, because the lighting is bad enough when you feel OK about yourself. I'd gone up a size, but it was not so much the weight that was new, it was my entire body shape. My waist was non-existent, my boobs were huge, and my bum had completely disappeared. I'd heard the phrase 'mum-bum' from a personal trainer on Instagram who had done a post encouraging mums to sign up to a bounce-back programme – which shouldn't be a thing. Some women find their bums go flat from hormones, their posture and muscle imbalances. But they come back. And you don't need someone telling you they can fix it overnight. You don't need to be fixed; you just need time. For that trip, I managed to find clothes that I felt OK in, like an oversized cardigan over a skirt so you couldn't see my tummy, and big jumpers covering my hips. It was almost like I was hiding being pregnant again.

The second night at dinner, we got chatting to the people on the table next to us. They were an older couple who had come for a staycation, and had just became grandparents themselves. Just as they were about to leave, the woman gave me a ten-pound note for Billie and my mum started welling up. I had no idea what was happening, but my mum explained to me it was called 'silvering the baby': a Scottish tradition from back in the day when someone would place a silver coin under a newborn baby's pillow to give them a financially secure future. This happened for my mum on my first holiday up to Scotland, too. We visited Port Appin in Oban when I was about two months old, around the same age Billie was when we went to Cromlix. We stopped off in Glasgow to see the relatives on my mum's side, and my great-granny Kelly, my mum's gran, gave me a 'silver' fifty-pence piece wrapped in tin foil. She also put an old silver sixpence in my chubby wee hand, which Mum still has somewhere. My great-aunties Carol and Lydia and my great-uncle Billy gave me 'silver coins' too, for good luck, and it even continued when we got to Oban. All the aunties and uncles lived on the same street in Rutherglen. Now, this sounds mad, but for my granny's generation this was the norm.

Another reason why we went up to Scotland was to go and see Dundee United and take Billie to her first match. Obviously we got her a babygro, vest, hat and bib for the occasion. I had her in the carrier, tucked up in my big coat that had an extra zip-up panel so she was totally covered. We were sitting at the top of the stadium, and she had her little ear defenders on so it wasn't too loud for her. She was the good-luck charm, with the team beating Ross County 3–0. We missed one of the goals for a bum change, but it was a very successful day out.

What was even more of a success – and just completely bizarre – was that Billie did her longest stint of sleep on that trip, going from 11 p.m. to 5 a.m. This was unheard of, and Steve and I looked at each other in complete disbelief that it had happened. The only reasonable explanation was that she needed to be in Scotland and a five-star hotel to sleep, so it was settled that we would just have to move in and leave our lives down south.

Just as we were – very reluctantly – going to the airport to head home, Rhiannon messaged me asking how I knew I had mastitis, and saying that she had a small, red lump starting to get bigger on her boob. I told her to ring 111 immediately and not leave it any longer.

Motherhood leads to inevitable changes in your body, and these extend beyond giving birth. While looking after your baby becomes your number-one priority, you also need to look after yourself and, crucially, listen to and get to know your body as it adapts. This means being aware of how you are feeling physically and mentally, and making sure you take care of your own health, if for no other reason than looking after yourself means you can look after your baby. But it also means recognising that your body won't be the same after giving birth, and no one should expect it to. I was under the impression that, after birth, you would immediately get your body back, but it's just not the case. Everything will be different, and that's OK. I was constantly changing emotionally and mentally, growing in ways I hadn't expected, and I had to learn not to get caught up in how I looked.

8

~~'You'll spoil that baby'~~
You Won't Create Bad Habits by Responding to Your Baby's Needs

When Billie was around three months old, the phrase 'the nights are long but the years are short' was being thrown around by anyone with older kids that I spoke to. I felt so guilty at this time, because I wanted the nights to be short and to get to that stage where you 'miss these days'! I couldn't quite get comfortable with the fact that I loved Billie but hated a lot of the things that went with being a new parent. The relentlessness of nappies, feeding, burping, being covered in sick, my boobs aching – it was a lot. What was worse was feeling guilty about not enjoying all of it, because I know that one day I would look back and kill to be exactly there. Or so this is what everyone told me.

We were getting out and about more and I was getting a little bit sick of doing the same lap of the park. (Although one thing I loved about where we lived in London at this time was that you could so often spot a celebrity in the park: when I was pregnant, Kit Harington walked past me and I swear on my life Billie started kicking, as if she knew it was a big deal. Steve saw Rosamund Pike at our local Pret; Alex's partner Ferg saw Phoebe Waller-Bridge outside the local wine shop. The best one was seeing James McAvoy in the pub with Billie, who gave him a big smile. I knew that the day I saw Paul Mescal, my set would be complete.)

It was around this time that the antenatal class mums had organised a reunion in the pub where we had the classes, and I was so excited about seeing everyone with their babies. However, this was a first taster of plans needing to be adaptable, because the morning of the meet-up, I had to take Billie to A&E.

Since she'd had her first round of vaccines, she hadn't done a poo in what was coming up to eleven days. By day seven, we called the GP and we were told to call 111 if nothing got moving by the weekend. It didn't, so I went to A&E on my own because Steve had to stay with Ruby, our dog, and I was the one with boobs.

One of my first memories is when my parents took me to High Wycombe A&E when I was about three, after I'd stepped on glass. My dad had left a glass on the floor by the sofa, and I hadn't seen it. There is obviously now a strict rule in their house and mine that no beverage can ever be on the ground. The cut was really deep, but I didn't need stitches. I remember the doctor using this purple-looking glue that came out of a huge syringe to stick the skin on the sole of my foot back together, but the thing I remember

You Won't Create Bad Habits by Responding to Your Baby's Needs

most is us bumping into another mum in the public eye and her daughter. They lived about twenty minutes from us, and her daughter must have been just a year old. She'd been stung by a bee, and my mum said she remembers the two of them just being really worried mums together. They just spoke about the two of us and didn't mention the music business or the mad world of TV at all. I was absolutely fine and so was her daughter. I left with a plaster on my foot, and her daughter with a very swollen thumb.

When Billie's name was called, we got put into one of the little rooms and they said that I had two options: going home and monitoring, or giving her a laxative there to 'help her out'. I very naively had messaged the antenatal group chat saying we were going to be a bit late to the reunion. I didn't want to go home only to have to come back the next day, so after chatting to Steve we decided to go with the laxative. I thought it would be like giving a baby Calpol, but it was a tiny little suppository that the nurse put up her bum. I was told to stay in the room for a bit before going home, and then later that day things would kick off. I can only explain it as a stream of poo coming out of her. I changed her twice, very quickly, but then decided the best course of action would be to put a puppy pad down and just let her go wild. (Puppy pads have been one of the best things we ever bought. Instead of washing Billie's bed sheets after every leak, we put one down between her mattress and mattress protector, one at her head for sick and one at her bum for wee and the inevitable poonami.)

At this stage, we'd only dealt with two really bad leaks, and funnily enough they were always on her dad.

She was once having a really cute nap on him, he was loving it, but I looked down and saw this stain that looked like a wet patch on his very dark T-shirt. There wasn't anything that could really be done then, so we waited until she woke up. It was the first time she was in leggings, and I moved them a bit to see how badly she had wet herself, but then the waistband of them had created a ring of poo. Steve then realised what the wet patch on him really was.

I have asked Mum, and apparently I never had poo explosions. My granny told me that in her day, it was such a faff. The nappies then were terry towelling, which was an absorbent square cloth, which you had to fold up into a nappy and then fasten with safety pins. If you had a boy, then you would have blue or green safety pins, and if you had a girl, pink. The green ladies' first piece of advice if your baby was crying was to check that the pins weren't sticking into them! The terry nappies had muslins as liners, but you'd need to wash both to reuse them. Granny had to boil them in a huge pot and then shove them in the bath with soapy water, because they didn't have a washing machine. If the nappy was really bad and could never come back to life, she would put it in the coal fire. Now it just goes in the dedicated nappy bin, and then it's Steve's job to empty it into the big bin.

Whenever I go to put one of Billie's dirty nappies in the bin, I always think of a story my mum told me. When her mum was changing my nappy when I was tiny, my mum thought something was wrong because she was taking ages, but really what happened was my granny couldn't work

You Won't Create Bad Habits by Responding to Your Baby's Needs

out the nappy bin, that you had to push the nappy down, and then twist and click the lid to cover it back up, ready for the next one. She was also used to nappy pins and not the sticky tape the modern ones had, and because she had covered her hands in nappy cream, that wasn't working for her either.

We were now two hours late for the reunion and I'd finally accepted the fact that we weren't going to make it. Judging by the rate of the fluid coming out of Billie, I think if this was still happening when we arrived, we would have been kicked out of the pub. Just as we were getting discharged, the doctor said that constipation is really normal in babies after getting their first round of vaccines, and the culprit is the Rotavirus – the same one she would have again at twelve weeks!

The new normal for my days was coming into full effect. My life, of course, now revolved around Billie, and I don't think that change is spoken about enough. Naturally, your life changes in huge ways after such a momentous event – but it changes in small ways, too. Every minute of the day, you have responsibility for another being entirely. Maybe you will miss these days full of responsibility, but it's OK to think you won't miss them, either. Scaring people about the hard bits to come is also not the way to support new parents going through it!

I made it my new thing to get out of the house every day and get some fresh air and a treat. But the amount of food I was eating was out of control. I thought after I'd given birth I would get onboard the keep-fit train and want to 'bounce back', but no one tells you how hungry you will be when breastfeeding. I still very much had a tummy, but could no longer tell if it was still my uterus shrinking or if the constant pastries were taking over. I was on a mission to find the best chocolate croissant in London, and decided to start small first, by visiting all the bakeries and shops near me. If it wasn't pastries, I was getting brownies, and if you get the small ones in packets of six or ten, for me, that counted as one! The absolute non-negotiable snack I would always get Steve to buy me whenever he left the house was Kellogg's Crunchy Nut Clusters. I can't even look at them now. I've always thought that if we ever have another baby I won't need to tell him I'm pregnant, I'll just pass a box to him.

I waited for Billie to have her first round of vaccines and to reach three months before going to any baby classes. The first thing we did was a sensory class, and it was terrifying. That was probably down to the woman taking the class, covering for the regular lady, and her treating it all a bit too seriously. The first song was for parents, and we were sat down in a circle, our babies lying on blankets in front of us. In the middle, there was a massive sequinned blanket (very RuPaul). We did some stretches and breathing exercises before moving on to a baby massage. We then had some more songs, and all held onto the blanket before lifting it up to reveal tummy-time island. Every week was a different theme, and because we were so close to Christmas, there were Santa hats, tinsel and tree decorations scattered around. The result was the best picture I have taken of Billie in her life, featuring a Santa hat and a very unhappy face. My own wee Grinch.

You Won't Create Bad Habits by Responding to Your Baby's Needs

I was the only mum there who had never been before, so I was really nervous. I hadn't been in a group like that on my own since I first moved to Singapore and went as a plus-one to a boat party. I didn't think that one through, because there was no way I could have left the boat if I didn't get along with anyone. Luckily, that was the day I met Jo and Charlie, and I can only imagine how boring life would be without them.

Because I was new, I was the only one in the class who didn't know the words to the songs, but Billie loved it. She wasn't fussed about what I was doing in the slightest and just wanted to look at the other babies.

That same week, I was supposed to have gone to see Black Coffee at Alexandra Palace with three of my friends. I remember telling my friend not to get me a ticket just in case I couldn't make it. Normally, if I couldn't make an event or a night out I'd be gutted, but this time I really didn't care. I loved my friends, of course, but the thought of being away from Billie was just completely unfeasible. Mainly because of my boobs.

Next on our new social calendar was baby swimming. Billie loved baths and water, so I knew she'd love swimming. I bought her a long-sleeved swimming costume, swim nappies, a new towel and a changing mat specifically for our pool trips. One very important tip with the swim nappies is to not keep them anywhere near the normal nappies. Jo told me that once, in the middle of the night when her baby had woken up, she wanted to keep the lights really dim, so when she changed him she reached for a nappy and then shoved him into bed with her. An hour or so later, she woke up in a pool of liquid, because she had put him in a swim nappy. They catch poo, but everything else just goes right through. What a way to learn that.

Some grannies were sitting behind the glass in the pool, watching the class. Kick-off was at 9.30 a.m., so there was no way my mum would be able to come and watch, but the gym was behind the seats and the TVs in there were showing ITV – so, technically, Granny was there the whole time. I thought I was being so clever and organised by wearing my swimming costume under my clothes, before realising I had packed everything for Billie but nothing for myself. That didn't happen again.

Baby yoga was also added to our agenda and, after a few weeks, I felt like I was slowly finding my village. (When I told my parents about baby yoga, they thought I was putting Billie in a downward dog position – but no, I do the yoga and Billie sleeps.) I had the mums from my antenatal class, and I had the new mums from all my other classes. The classes turned out to be for me, as well as Billie. I needed them too. Your days change so much that you need other people around you going through the same thing. You need people to text in the middle of the night during a meltdown, and to ask, 'Is this normal?' for the thousandth time. You need a village around you, whether they are family or friends (old or new). Find your people, and you'll find a little bit of sanity in the new ways you're living your life.

For my granny, her neighbours (some of whom were family) acted as her village. She told me how she would leave my mum's little brother, Graham, to nap in his cot on the street, and she would go up to her flat and do

You Won't Create Bad Habits by Responding to Your Baby's Needs

housework. That was normal then, but I could not imagine doing it now. With my mum working and the baby classes generally being in the morning, she never got to meet other mums in the same boat as her. I don't know what I would have done without those social situations, because it's during them that you realise you're not on your own. Not having that exchange of information with people going through the same thing must have been very isolating. It was isolating for me, and I knew people with babies Billie's age!

My mum told me that she feels as though she missed out on having that support system, but on the other hand is really glad that social media didn't exist. She liked learning on the job, but missed the opportunity to make new friends and get the confidence to be able to talk about the highs and lows of raising a baby. None of my mum's friends at that time had children, and there were no other babies on either side of the family, nor any signs of them arriving. My mum's 'village' was very, very small. She had my dad, her mum on the end of the phone, Dr Hilary at work and Aunty Joyce about an hour away for babysitting. My two nannies had invaluable advice, but she told me when I started writing this book that she always questioned whether she was 'doing it right'. I think this is something every mum fears, across every generation. At this early point in time, I really do think only other mums understand what you're going through – and I say this with a lot of hesitation, but new dads just don't get it. Mainly, I think that's because of all the insane hormones you have swirling around inside.

With all of the lovely new hormones from having a baby pumping different emotions through my body, the one that

I definitely didn't know was coming was the rage. My rage was directed towards Steve. Most of the time, I knew I had taken something small and made it into a way bigger deal. For example, I got incredibly angry that he was taking such a long time to fill my water bottle up, or to grab me a muslin. Minutes could feel like hours. Although, there were things that he did that were quite valid for me to be mad about. Three weeks after my C-section, I remember asking for his help to get up from the sofa. He asked if it still hurt. I'd had major surgery.

It quickly became clear to me that instinct is a very real thing for mums. You're a mum as soon as you see the two blue lines on the pregnancy test, but dads have to learn to be a parent. It's a job for them that they're given overnight, and that's their life completely changed. Although there may be some changes for them during the pregnancy, like preparing for baby to arrive, it's not the same as the changes that take over a mum as soon as she becomes pregnant.

My dad spent a lot more time with me because he was freelance rather than working a normal nine-to-five, which must have sped the whole process up for him and allowed him to gain confidence in parenting quicker.

Something Steve and I fought about at this time was his running. It's really common for partners to pick up a new hobby around the time of a pregnancy. Steve had started running when we first got together, but now it was taking on a life of its own. He was training for a marathon when I was pregnant, but I thought that was going to be it. He had gone on to sign up for a bunch of half-marathons, the

You Won't Create Bad Habits by Responding to Your Baby's Needs

Manchester marathon and then an ultramarathon where he was going to be running 100km a few weeks after Billie turned one. He would get out of the house often for runs, which he needed to do for his own mental health, but I was then left alone. Some nights were worse than others, and I needed help. I really needed rest, but having an hour's nap in the morning before he went to work couldn't happen because he 'needed' to run. Cue his next corker of saying that exercise was 'the only time he got to himself'. In response, I listed off the things I could no longer do that he still could: go to the loo, shower, wash my hair, dry my hair, make something to eat, have a drink, stand up or sit down.

I internalised a lot of my anger because I didn't want to be thought of as a nag. We were fully in the roommate phase of our relationship: sleeping in different rooms, and not eating together as we had to take it in turns. We were just getting by, day by day. Any time we tried to sit down for dinner together, Billie would, without fail, have a meltdown and need a cuddle. We both hated her crying and wanted to comfort her, but for me it felt like my entire body was on fire. I couldn't cope with it, so I'd always pick her up and try to soothe her, which nine times out of ten meant a feed.

Steve and my dad would be considered very 'hands-on' compared to dads in my granny's day. 'Hands-on' is a phrase I hate, because it's not a way anyone would describe a mother. I feel this term is used to glorify a role that mums do every day, but without getting any credit. Men are classed as 'babysitters' for looking after their own children!

For my granny, my grandad did absolutely nothing to help with my mum, but that's what was expected of men of that generation. He wasn't even allowed in the room when my mum was born. My dad, like Steve, changed the first nappy of his child, something I don't think my grandad ever did. It now seems this is a rite of passage for new dads, and he actually had to show me how to do it once I was back on my feet. We had practised on dolls in the antenatal class, but it's never the same. My C-section scar was at the same level as the changing table, so for those first few weeks, I had to step back and bend over so I could reach.

Despite me sometimes feeling frustrated, Steve was the best. He made snack bowls for me for the long nights, which were so thoughtful, and he always took pictures of Billie when he had her so I didn't miss anything.

My mum told me that Dad slept in the spare room for a bit, just like Steve did, so he would then have the energy to look after me during the day. The first few weeks after my mum was born, she and my granny stayed with Granny Mac, who took total control over everything. If it wasn't for Granny breastfeeding, she would have been completely cut off from Mum. My granny and grandad soon rushed back to their one room in the Gorbals to spend time together as a family.

We were slowly finding our new normal, and one thing that I knew meant we were coming out of the trenches was that I had started sleeping a bit more deeply. I was dreaming again, and dreaming means you're sleeping.

You Won't Create Bad Habits by Responding to Your Baby's Needs

THINGS NEEDED FOR A NEWBORN (0–3 MONTHS)

- Puppy pads
- iPad to watch shows in bed, no earphones necessary
- Face spray to wake yourself up in the night
- Sugar-free Red Bull

9

~~'sleep when the baby sleeps'~~

Sleep When You Can

The first time someone said this to me was a day after Billie's birth, when the consultant came to check on my scar. Billie was sleeping in her wee plastic cot next to me, and I just thought it would be that easy: when she's sleeping – I'll just sleep. Little did I know she would not want to sleep independently again, and instead would be on either Steve or me for the next few weeks. When she was on Steve or starting to sleep more on her own, I then had the options of going for a shower, eating something or just generally doing something for myself. I didn't think it was worth getting all cosy in bed and going to sleep if I'd be up again in minutes if she needed food.

It felt like I had just got Billie used to sleeping in her cot beside our bed, rather than solely on me or her dad, when the four-month sleep regression videos started popping up on my social media feed. I swear the apps were tracking what stage we were at! I wouldn't have known this was a thing unless it was for social media and, to be honest, I could have done without it. I received far too much information (all conflicting) on what to expect, what to do and why it was happening. Essentially, from what I gathered, it's babies adjusting from newborn to adult sleep cycles and is a normal part of their development.

I knew a few mums who did the 'cry it out' method or 'Ferberizing' from the get-go, and some who did it after a few months of trying everything and nothing working. Dr Richard Ferber introduced the tactic of increasing the time intervals before you respond to your baby crying, which is meant to eventually lead them to self-soothe and sleep independently.

My granny lived in a one-bedroom flat, so there was no such thing as a separate nursery for my mum, or her brother when he arrived six years later. Mum and her brother always slept in their cots, and leaving them to cry and soothe themselves was what mums were told to do. My great-aunt Josephine was told that letting babies cry was good for their lungs. When my granny had my mum, she didn't have any pressure of going back to work, and when my mum had me, she was lucky that she didn't sleep much anyway because of her job, so she was used to it! Many mums now, of course, are having to go back to work after a few months, or are freelance and are still working, so I can totally see how this method to get their babies to sleep through the night would be an option. Josephine and Granny didn't go back to work until their babies were at school, and even then it was part-time.

When I was born in the nineties, it was still the standard advice to let babies cry themselves to sleep. When I was tiny, my mum would hold me and rock me to sleep, and if

I was then put down in my wee crib, I would start crying. My mum or dad would either rock me to sleep again or walk around with me. My dad would take me round the garden for hours, and I was born in June, so it didn't get dark for ages. My mum said that I was a good wee baby, never had any tummy troubles or colic, but was a wee bugger at going to sleep. It was as though I didn't want to miss anything. It seems that this characteristic had indeed been passed down to Billie.

A new classic from Steve was introduced on the topic of sleep, that 'we were the same level of tired'. This coming from the man who slept in the spare room for eight hours uninterrupted! His reasoning was that he was in 'sleep debt' from the newborn days, and was now constantly trying to catch up. I just gave him a look rather than saying anything back, and I could see the panic in his eyes . . .

Although the women from the antenatal group had all formed really close bonds and our own group chats, this wasn't the case for the men. I think it's so important for dads to have an outlet, too. Like me, Steve was the first of his friends to have a baby, so he needed some dads to talk to. Trying to get men to talk to one another about how they feel is extremely hard. One of the reasons I was so happy we were having a girl is because she would have female friendships, like I did. I love Steve, but the way I speak and laugh with Amber, Jen, Charlie and Jo is just on another level! Steve was preaching to the wrong choir by complaining to me about being tired, which of course he was, but he needed people that got it, like I did with my mums.

Not getting to sleep is all part of having a baby, I'd learnt that by this point. Billie was more than likely going to have sleep regressions, so I didn't want to get caught up in tracking how long she was sleeping for, how many naps she was having, and even where she was sleeping. She wasn't a good sleeper anyway, but Billie's sleep habits completely changed when we hit the four-month sleep regression. We were back to square one in effect, as she refused to nap unless she was on someone again, and she hated her cot. I could get her to fall asleep on me, completely out for the count, and then had to do this very graceful manoeuvre of melting myself into the bed to put her down next to me. This was the beginning of co-sleeping for us. For Billie, this stage lasted two weeks, and it was rough.

Nearing December, our flat was on the market and we had found a house we wanted to buy. Our estate agent said to not have any clutter for the pictures and for the house viewings, so we decided not to put decorations up, which was a bit devastating. I was so excited to get the flat beautiful for Billie's first Christmas, but, to be honest, I don't know where I was expecting to find the time to do that.

At this time of year, the nights were dark and cosy, the decorations twinkled and there was so much food. Storing my milk in the fridge in the middle of the night was actually quite lovely now, with the Christmas tree greeting me on the way to the kitchen. I don't believe that you can only celebrate Christmas on the day, so pigs in blankets are very much a late-November staple in our house.

Having to get the house ready for viewings was stressful and time-consuming enough, but when you add a new baby

Sleep When You Can

and a dog to clean up after, it was too much. (Especially when estate agents ask for access at 8 a.m. so a couple can come and have a look before going to work.)

With my parents being just over an hour's drive away, we were spending a lot more time there, and our worst night to date was with my mum and dad present. I was demented. Billie was up every hour and nothing was working. We think she had started teething around this point, and we were told to give her teething powder and teething gel. If that didn't work, we would give her Calpol. I had no idea she was teething until I had a chat with one of the mums at baby swimming. She asked how things were going and I said they were OK, but that Billie was feeding more than normal and drooling a lot. I thought the signs for teething would be Billie shoving everything in her mouth and gnawing away at anything she could get her hands on, but apparently these were also signs. Swimming mum said her baby had started at three months, and my other friend (who is a Norland Nanny – very handy) told me that some babies are even born with teeth!

The teething powder we used came in a tiny sachet and was white, so naturally we called it 'baby cocaine'. We would get Billie's dummy from her so it was wet or suck it ourselves, and then shove it in the pouch so it was covered, a bit like those Dip Dab lollipops I used to get at school.

My granny used to put teething rings in the freezer for my mum and her brother, which were just coming out at that time. My great-granny (Mum's grandma) told Mum to put whisky on my gums and my dummy, as it numbed the pain and would put me to sleep. My great-granny did it for my grandad, my mum's dad, who was the grumpiest baby ever born. He cried until he was two years old, and the staff at the hospital said they'd never been happier to see a baby go home. Bizarrely, Great-Granny Kelly had more kids after him, and he was the oldest of four. My mum obviously never gave me booze, but she did accept another piece of Great-Granny Kelly's advice and gave me a clean frozen muslin to chew on, which I apparently loved.

During our night of hell at mum and dad's, I was going through the ritual of making sure Billie's nappy wasn't full, feeding her, burping her and then checking all over again. We were both crying at that point, and just as I was about to give up and get my mum, she came knocking on my door. I didn't need scientific proof that men can't hear a baby crying if they're sleeping, it was happening right in front of my eyes. Both my dad and Steve were sleeping soundly, while all the girls were up (including Ruby!). My mum was listing things that could be making Billie so upset and keeping her from sleeping, and I snapped at her, saying I had tried everything. I'd never talked to her like that before, but I was on no sleep and under so much stress trying to make Billie happy. We had definitely become closer since I found out I was pregnant, and even more so once Billie was here. There was a level of understanding I only got when Billie was born.

It was now around 4 a.m., and Mum was up for work in an hour anyway, so she took Billie for a walk around the house, which calmed her down. I always felt guilty when my mum would come and help in those early months, because it was either way before her time to get up for work and when she should be sleeping, or on her day off, when she could actually sleep!

I decided it was time to really track Billie's naps. She was doing one in the morning, then two or three short ones in the afternoon. I tried to get her not to sleep past five so we could do her bedtime at seven, but if she was exhausted, I'd just let her sleep. I felt awful about waking her up from a nap, so I just never did it!

I downloaded an app which was recommended by the mums in the antenatal group. It readjusts the time of the naps babies need by how much they've slept in the night. I needed some control in my life, and even if it didn't work and she didn't sleep better, I thought the placebo effect of using an app would help at this point . . .

I used it religiously for about two weeks before I found myself going slightly mad. One day, Billie refused to go down for her third nap, and the app suggested we just do her bedtime routine at 5 p.m. This logic just wasn't working for me, as I knew she'd then be up a few hours later, and stay up for eternity. I went with my instinct and stuck to doing her bedtime at the same time, and miraculously she slept. At the end of the day, it was an app telling me what to do and not someone I trusted, so I did what would have been unthinkable for me before Billie and listened to myself! She was up a few hours later anyway, but easily went back down. I was in a foul mood before this as I thought the two naps a day were what was needed, but really, every day was different. Babies just make no sense.

She was getting into more of a rhythm now of going to sleep at 7 p.m., and Steve and I now had guaranteed time to ourselves when she first went down. We didn't know what to do with ourselves! I remember getting really into darts and staying up late to watch Luke Littler win the world championships.

On Christmas Eve, we always go out for lunch. I wanted to look nice, but nothing fit me apart from an old black jumpsuit. It had a zip going all the way up the front, and just as we sat down it decided to burst. I had to wear my dad's jumper for the rest of the meal, and I just looked and felt so out of place. It felt like I had tried to make an effort and the world was against me. I'd specifically worn something I could breastfeed in, that wasn't a massive jumper and leggings. Billie, on the other hand, was in her brand-new red Christmas dress with white tights, a Santa hat and gorgeous gold ballet pumps that had big ribbon bows.

Steve had a few days off work before and after Christmas, and I think I would have lost my mind if he wasn't there to help. There's the usual stuff it's nice to have a break from, like nappies, and getting him to take Billie for a walk so I could nap, but no one really speaks about the mental load you can't share when your partner is at work. When it's just you on your own, you're the only one who knows when she last did a poo, and when you need to feed her. If you have anxiety like I did, it just multiplies everything. The only person you have to talk to all day is this tiny human who's not even discovered they have hands yet. When Steve went back to work, it was almost like going back to school (which I didn't enjoy). You'd had all this lovely family time, and then it was back to being sensible – being the grown-up.

Sleep When You Can

Billie was due her next round of vaccinations on New Year's Eve, and I had a little cry this time, but nothing like my full meltdown the time before. What didn't help was another mum in the waiting room saying that this was the easy stage, because it certainly didn't feel like it. Comments like these just aren't helpful for any new mum, even if they're coming from a good place. No one knows what anyone else is going through; no one can be sure that a new parent hasn't experienced a truly awful first few months with their baby. What I'd love to suggest is that we're all just a little more thoughtful and kinder to new parents – it doesn't take much at all to make or break someone's day. I wasn't locked into routines at this point, and didn't yet have to think about weaning and crafting three meals a day, or making sure she hadn't crawled into the oven or eaten a battery! I felt guilty for having felt so awful during this stage, and for finding it so hard. This was mainly down to lack of sleep, which is why being supported during this time and knowing you might go through it is so important. I thought at the time that if I had more energy, I'd be flying through the whole motherhood thing, which is why sleep during those early weeks and months is such an important thing to talk about openly.

I didn't really notice the time between Christmas and New Year because it felt like wading through a fog – and every day for the first few months was exactly like that. I couldn't tell you what day it was, and it didn't really matter. We didn't make any plans for celebrating New Year's Eve, apart from forcing Steve to watch the Scottish coverage, but I only made it to 10 p.m. before going to bed. Weirdly for her, Billie didn't wake up, so I was in a pickle about whether I should 'dream feed' her or just let her be. A dream feed involved feeding her when she was just wriggling and thinking about getting up. One of my family friends who has three boys, one that's my godson, told me about this, and instead of turning to Google, I just listened to her. She said to not actively wake Billie up and not turn on the lights, but pick her up, feed her, have a wee cuddle with no burp, and then pop her back in the crib. This friend is the one that also told me about trying a dummy first rather than your boob if they wake up in the night. (The word 'if' there made me laugh.) This was one of the first times I'd trusted someone who wasn't an 'expert in their field', and the first time I realised that, actually, other mums *are* the experts. Turning to those who have done it before is exactly the right thing to do. Whether their advice or stories are helpful is one thing, but learning you're not alone is exactly what you need at any stage of motherhood.

On her first New Year's Eve, I like to think Billie had some sense of what was going on, because her first wake-up was at five minutes to midnight, and we both ended up listening to some of the fireworks going off. It was this time the previous year we had found out we were having a baby and, even with my mind racing then, I didn't think where I would be on that night a year on, and what I'd be doing. It was still so surreal to me that she was here and, even though at this point I really was up constantly, I felt so lucky that she was the one keeping me up.

When the new year arrived, it was time to go back to London and for Steve to go back to work, and luckily all our baby classes were back on too, so Billie's schedule was fully booked! Monday we had baby sensory, Tuesday we had baby yoga, Wednesday was baby swimming and then Thursday was our free day. I needed something booked in, as I didn't like not knowing what was happening. I think this is due to how isolating motherhood can be. I needed to be around people, and I needed to be around other mums.

You would have thought that after all this time I would be so on it with what to pack for baby swimming, especially after not taking any pants for me and doing a funny walk home. This time, I had got into the pool and my boobs felt soggy. I had left my cotton reusable breast pads in my costume – thank the lord they never made an escape. I had visions of them floating in the shallow baby pool . . . From then on, I went back to the sticky disposable breast pads that were less thick.

When I was walking through the park one day, one of the mums who had been at the class was pushing her pram and walking alongside her own mum, who had come to watch. They were arguing about something, which is putting it nicely. The new mum was having a proper go at her mum about an upcoming holiday they were having, and all I could do was feel so incredibly sad at witnessing it. I didn't fully know the situation, of course, but at a time in your life when you hope families will come together, or create new connections, it's massively hard when that doesn't happen. With so many emotions and hormones, especially during the early stages, it's hard not to take feelings out on others when you take into account the lack of sleep, especially on those closest to you.

MOTHER TO MOTHER

I don't know if it was because I was going out all the time with Billie, but she would now only sleep in her pram. I wanted her to be able to sleep anywhere. While it was nice not being restricted to staying indoors for naps, the weather in January was bleak, and going out three times a day was rough. I could do her first nap on the way to something in the morning, like a class or to get a pastry, and then a walk back home would equal another nap, but that third one was a killer. I think the fact that we were living in a basement flat was part of the problem, because I had to lug the pram up the stairs every time . . . I know what you might be thinking: pop her in the pram in the flat and walk her up and down the hallway, but this child had the ability to know we weren't outside, and I wasn't freezing cold or miserable enough!

I tried to make it a real positive, being out constantly, and so bought myself a new raincoat. It was more like a poncho, and I'd bought it after a stream of targeted ads on Instagram. I'd succumbed to a dark green leopard-print design, and thought I looked cool – until Steve took a picture of me coming in the door. I had my hair in a very messy bun on top of my head, under the hood on of this very oversized garment. I looked like a human condom. Billie, on the other hand, was in a vest, bodysuit, a pink woolly hat and her starfish blanket that she was folded into like a burrito (one of the best purchases we ever made, and something I get for any friend having a baby). She wasn't fussed about the rain cover early on, but it got to be really distracting for her when she was trying to sleep. Because the pram could double as a car seat, the cover draped over the front and made it look as if she was in a pod for space travel. She kept grabbing it as if she wanted to escape, and then never really relaxed with it. For her 'main sleep', as I liked to call it, we were now letting her do her first stint of sleep in her cot, so from 7 p.m. to 11 p.m., and then she would come into the bed with us. She wasn't rolling yet, but we popped her in the middle of me and Steve anyway.

When things started to settle a bit after the regression, Steve booked a roast at the pub where we'd had our first date. I can't recommend how important it is to still do these things and not be scared about how your baby will be if you go out. People can choose to not have a baby in their lives, but they can't choose to have a baby-free world. This is something I decided I would repeatedly tell myself, like a mantra, before taking Billie out somewhere. Billie slept the whole time we were there, right next to our table, and the family next to us even said how lucky we were to have such an angel. She was, of course, an angel, but a total monkey at home. But I'd much rather she be a dream in public and a nightmare when it's just us . . .

She was getting chunkier, with rolls on her arms and legs, but she was also really long. It definitely wasn't coming from my side of the family, and we kept joking she would grow up to be six foot six. Whenever I got her weighed, the health visitor would check what percentile she was in, and some mums would always want to chat about this too. I didn't really take any notice of it, probably because Billie was in a good range and growing really well. She was in the 95th percentile.

Billie was now sitting up properly, and this was her first milestone that made me think she was becoming a proper little person. I couldn't watch my shows in bed anymore, because she'd started noticing them, and I obviously didn't want her associating feeding with the Real Housewives of New York screaming at each other. I'd popped a huge muslin over her play gym that was on our big sofa so we could still have the TV on but not have her watch it. I did make exceptions, though, when Granny's show was on.

10

'We didn't do that in my day, and mine turned out fine'

Do What Works For You

My granny would definitely say that a lot of things have got so much better since she first became a mum. Disposable nappies being the main thing. The one thing she did say to my mum about my parenting was that I had too much stuff. Too many clothes and too many toys! I think people just didn't have as much stuff in her day, and there wasn't actually that much to buy. Kids played outside all day until it was dark. She said to 'let kids get bored so they can use their imagination'.

As I've said, the biggest change between generations I've seen is the idea of letting your baby cry. My granny let my mum and uncle cry, just because that's what you did. 'Self-soothing' became less and less popular after the eighties, and studies have shown that doing this for long periods of time can have negative long-term impacts on a baby's emotional and brain development. They will be crying for a reason, and they're dependent on you to manage their stress. Laura told me to check if Billie was hungry, needed a bum change or needed a cuddle. If nothing worked, pop her down in her cot, somewhere safe, then go into the kitchen and run the tap for a break before going back in.

We had almost reached the six-month mark and Billie was a very content baby. I felt like I had just got lucky, but everyone said it was because we were doing such a good job with her. I obviously can't take a compliment, so just smiled awkwardly every time. My mum had the opposite, with people telling her she was lucky. A lot of it comes down to the fact that if babies feel safe and loved, they're going to be happy. Some babies, of course, are happier than others, but that guidance is still there.

On the other hand, there is nothing like weaning to show how years change and advice develops. What filled me with a lot of anxiety at this point was starting to introduce Billie to real foods and the risk of her choking. I felt like I couldn't enjoy the stage I was in or soak anything up, because the next new thing was around the corner. It's something I brought up a lot with the nurse I was still seeing every other week. I had it in my head that we would definitely need to wean Billie soon. Her advice was to wait for the six month-mark, even though she was showing signs that she was ready, as there would be no harm in making sure I was ready too. I forced myself to watch the St John Ambulance video of what to do if your baby is choking. To this day, I cannot imagine anything worse, but I had to be prepared. There was a side of me that wanted to feel organised and ready, but also a side that knew she wouldn't need to feed off me as much. This was the first gut-wrenching stage of Billie being more independent. It's the whole point of raising them, but no one speaks about how hard it is on you.

I had seen social media videos with titles like, 'Signs your baby is ready for weaning.' One of these signs was the baby holding their head up by themselves and sitting up. Another one was how babies will start looking at what you're eating and take a real interest in it. There was a lot to digest (literally) and I felt so guilty again at this point for finding breastfeeding so hard, as now I had to prepare actual food! In terms of feeding her before, I'd just been able to whip my boobs out.

A few people had told me that when Billie started having solids, her sleep would get a lot better. She was still up in the night an average of three or four times, but a quick feed and she was right back to sleep. Getting to six months also meant that Billie had technically outgrown her bedside cot and was ready to be in her own room. I was not ready for this, even though she was only doing her first stint of sleep in the bedside cot before coming in with us. My back was ready for it, though, because I was taking on the shape of a Quaver. The longer she slept on her own, the longer I knew she could go without food, so that's when I started to think about reducing her feeds in the night and substituting them with cuddles, but we were a long way off this. A bit like the weaning, her sleeping in her own room signalled her growing up and not needing me as much.

I had to take Billie to the GP one week, and just as we were leaving, the doctor said I needed to start weaning her. She was a week or two away from six months, so that's when I decided that enough was enough, I was going to do my research and everything would be fine, because it had to be. It's not like I wasn't ever going to let her eat anything, so we may as well start now!

I obviously went back to my gospel group chat of Jo and Charlie and asked them about weaning, and they reassured me that it would be totally fine. Jo actually came round to see us and recommended I follow Charlotte Stirling-Reed on Instagram, so I bought her book and downloaded the Solid Starts app. (The app lets you search for a particular food and then shows you how to serve it at each age, which I found really useful. For example, with toast, from six months you can cut it up into strips, then from nine months into bite-sized square pieces, then from eighteen months however you want.) This is when information online really helped me, when it was recommended by someone I trusted.

My mum had 'Ask Jeeves', which was very much in its infancy, and she didn't like using it. She got all her info from Jacqueline, Dr Hilary, her GP and, of course, her mum. There was no book she faithfully followed; she learnt on the job. If Mum had her time again now, she would have googled a *lot* of things, and I've seen her doing it with Billie. There was one really hot day when Billie was drinking more water than normal that caused my mum to reach for the phone and start googling. Terrifying results came up about sending their wee kidneys into overdrive, alongside comments from other people saying not to worry at all. After that episode, Mum decided she was very happy she couldn't easily look things up with me.

One thing Jo did say was that Billie would be more regular in the poo department when she started solids. At one point, after a call with the GP and 111, I was back to

Do What Works For You

the same A&E department we'd been to before, as it had been eleven days since her last movement. I didn't feel as worried this time going back to hospital as I'd been there before and for the exact same reason. I just expected them to stick the same tiny tablet up her bum and she would let rip. The doctor told me that I needed to understand Billie's rhythm better before coming into the hospital, which annoyed me a little bit because her rhythm was all over the place and the literal reason why we were there. I knew she hadn't been in an accident, she wasn't in any pain, and there were other babies there who needed to be seen too, but I was still worried about her.

Apart from cot death, my mum's big health worry for me was chickenpox, which I got twice. People then used to have 'pox parties' where catching it was encouraged, so children were intentionally exposed to it so they could have it and then be done with it. I have a scar on my nose from itching one of the scabs off, and my mum said I used to cry and cry in the night. I couldn't imagine Billie being in any kind of pain like that, and we are so lucky now that there's a vaccine for it. For my granny, the main worry back then was childhood diseases like mumps, polio and measles. My mum was vaccinated against polio, which came in 1955, but the vaccinations for measles didn't come until 1968, and it was 1988 for mumps.

We got home from the hospital and I put Billie to sleep and thought it was maybe all going to come into fruition during the night, but still nothing. The next morning I went to change her, and as I opened up her nappy, she delightfully did a fart, which meant all the poo (eleven days' worth) splattered all the way up my pyjamas and onto my neck. It was the first time in my life I've frozen and not really known what to do. Steve was out walking Ruby, so I grabbed some wipes to manage most of it, got her cleaned up properly and hopped in the shower. Showering on my own was a thing of the past unless someone else was in the flat to hold Billie, so I set up a play mat on the floor with some toys and extra blankets so I could have her in the room with me. I then discovered the laundry basket way too late. I got about a good two weeks out of her sitting in it before she figured out a way of standing up.

I didn't take her not moving for granted, but it was during one of our baby yoga sessions when I experienced feeling for the first time like I was being judged. Billie was sitting up on the mat we used for the yoga, and I'd gone to get a muslin from the pram that was inches away from her. I turned my back for one second and heard the biggest thud. She had fallen back and smacked her head on the floor. I thought it was all fine at first, but it was just a delayed cry. It was guttural, and I think due mainly to shock as the mat was squishy. One of the other mums saw and just didn't say anything. The silence was awful. She might not have been even thinking anything negative about it, but I assumed she was judging me – I think because *I* was really judging me. How on earth could I have let that happen? She had never done that before and I'd stupidly left Billie sitting up without a cushion or anything behind her. I cried as uncontrollably as her, and thank God for Randa, the teacher, who was there to give us both a cuddle.

My mum told me that I fell off the changing table when I was weeks old. She had turned round to get something,

Do What Works For You

and she still doesn't know how it happened, as I wasn't moving yet. The room had a thick carpet and it was not a big drop, so the tears – both mine and Mum's – were all down to shock. Accidents happen and every day is a new learning experience, for both you and your baby. Your biggest judge (outside of motherhood, too) is usually yourself, so give yourself a break and encourage other mums you know to do the same.

At this time, I took myself to the osteopath after speaking to one of my mum-friends about whether she had done any scar massage. We'd both had C-sections, and I was told that from six weeks I could start using creams or oils to massage my scar. It was coming up to six months since the birth, and I hadn't even looked at it yet, let alone touched it. When my friend said she had been to an ostepath and the therapist had not only showed her how to do the scar massage, but also sorted her back out, I was sold. I'm so glad I did it, and I wouldn't have known this was a thing unless I spoke to my friend. Going back a few years to when Charlie gave birth, the knowledge around scar massage just wasn't shared. You can now get full 'Mummy MOT' appointments that include a full postural screening, pelvic-floor muscle assessment, abdominal muscle exam to check for any separation, and screening for bladder, bowel or sexual dysfunction. I feel that this is something that should maybe be introduced to the very basic six-week check you get if you've had a C-section.

One of the worst parts of my mum's recovery was the first wee. Haemorrhoids also just come with the territory, and we both loved the Victoria Wood story that, when she gave birth, she told her mum to knit two hats! My mum didn't have painkillers because she was breastfeeding and was worried about how they would affect me, which was something I didn't even think of, but I feel that going without couldn't have been an option for me, as I'd been sliced open.

When I was about a week old, Mum and Dad had taken me out, and Dad was proudly carrying me around and accepting all the compliments about how adorable I was. Meanwhile, my mum was waddling behind, feeling as though her insides were going to fall out. My friend Jo experienced this too, and recommended I get a belly binder. I think people see these as something mums use to get their figures back, but I used it to feel like I had some support. It really helped with my posture, too. It was a really hot summer when I was born, and my mum was boiling hot, itchy, sore and knackered. I was lucky that Billie was born at the start of autumn, so I could hide under oversized jumpers and not feel too out of sorts.

My granny said she bounced back after the birth quickly because she was so young, although she did say she had a wee bit of a tummy. She said the key to getting her figure back was taking my mum on long walks in the pram, with her favourite loop being all around Glasgow Green.

When it came to weaning, I felt as prepared as I could have been. I had bought a classic bib, plus a sleeved bib that had a pocket along the bottom for escaping food. I also got spoons, bowls and the cutest sippy cup with Winnie-the-Pooh on it. The spoons were bizarre, with flat heads and grips all over them. This was for the early days and getting Billie used to holding one. (I definitely bought way too many of them for how much they were actually used.)

My mum wrote a book on weaning, but had absolutely no idea you couldn't give babies water or honey. It was never something she was told not to do by the GP or health visitor at the time. She had a health visitor who came round once or twice when they brought me home to check I was OK, but there wasn't the 'green lady' like her mum had. You had to ask for help if you needed it. There were no drop-in clinics at community or children's centres like there are now. Not having access to these resources and communities seems completely alien to me, and I have no idea what I would have done without them. It's still not a given for mums everywhere, and I did wonder if it was because we lived in London that we had all this at our fingertips.

I would always have porridge with honey for my breakfast, so when I was planning on making it for Billie, I just thought we could have that together. From 2005 in the UK, though, the warning 'unsuitable for infants under 12 months' was on almost every jar of honey sold – the same year I turned eleven and we moved to Scotland so I could start secondary school, so I definitely missed the boat. Honey actually became another thing to worry about in the late 1970s following infant botulism being diagnosed for the first time. This is a life-threatening, and very rare, illness caused by babies under one ingesting *Clostridium botulinum* bacteria[*] (very science-y), which produces a neurotoxin that leads

---

[*] https://www.theguardian.com/science/2005/aug/25/health.society
https://www.nhs.uk/conditions/botulism/

to muscle weakness, difficulty breathing and swallowing, and if untreated can lead to paralysis that spreads down the body from the head to the legs. Once babies pass the age of one, the body has developed defences against the resistant form of the bacteria. Honey is a sugar, so avoiding it for that reason is maybe easier to get your head around. It certainly was for me. I had a rule with Billie of no sugar and no salt, as much as I could help it.

I was really excited to give Billie water with solid food. I started with a beaker, which she immediately loved, and then we worked our way up to a sippy cup. We were a long way from using a straw, but she was not interested in her sippy cup for months, then one day just picked it up on her own and she was off. That was when Billie was six months, but my mum was giving me water way before that.

My mum said weaning me was relatively easy because I gave everything a go and loved my grub. She would cook broccoli and spinach together, like I do, mash them up and pop them into ice-cube trays so it was easier for tea at night or during the week. My dad would make my tea a lot while Mum was doing her homework for the next day. The two of us then went to bed around the same time, about 7 p.m., and then she'd get up and leave for work, handing me over to Dad or placing me in my cot if I allowed it.

Steve's mum came over the first time I gave Billie solid food, and it was really lovely to have her there for this huge milestone. I used our food processor to blitz some boiled broccoli and mixed it with some breast milk, and also gave her a tiny little floret as finger food in case she wanted to nibble on it. (Not that she had any teeth. We were really going through the baby cocaine at this point, and had to resort to Calpol a few nights in a row just to calm her down.)

It seemed from talking to my granny and great-aunt Josephine that introducing babies to solids hasn't massively changed. Mashed-up veggies and fruit were what they used too, but how they did it was slightly different. Josephine was living in Germany when weaning her two boys, and she was told to cut a bigger hole in the bottle teat and put carrot juice in the milk, which might have been the norm there. She'd put mashed banana in this way too, so they were drinking their solids. Then they just used veggies mashed with a fork, not a food processor.

My mum first tried tiny amounts of expressed milk with baby rice, and then mashed-up rusks, which were really easy for me to eat. She moved onto mashed-up chicken and rice, and fish, which I really liked, and eventually red meat, but nothing smoked like bacon or any processed or ready-made meals (apart from the occasional baby jar). My granny gave my mum jars when she was eighteen months, and they were a total revelation then. My mum and her brother would also get tiny tins of carrots and glasses of pudding. Pudding would be fruit though, not anything sweet, and Josephine said that they'd get their pudding after their nap after lunch.

The first ten days of weaning with Billie were each focused on trying one food, and by day four (aubergine) Billie was loving it. It was such a turning point, as she wasn't that bothered until then, with nothing really going in. Patience and perseverance, like with everything baby, were key. Charlotte Stirling-Reed told me: 'You wouldn't expect your baby to learn how to crawl or walk in a couple of days, so you shouldn't expect them to be experts in eating.' I was halfway through following Charlotte's book before realising my mum had her own I could have used! It was published nearly thirty years ago, and I wanted to have the most up-to-date information, but I did look through it. Mum was asked to write a book on weaning based on her own experience with me. She co-wrote it with the aptly named Anita Bean, a trained nutritionist, who checked all the recipes and her advice, and also came up with her own ideas. At that time in the early nineties, there weren't that many books written from the point of view of a 'normal' mum rather than an expert, and the book did really well. Parents would stop Mum to tell her how easy it was to understand and how simple the recipes were. Mum's favourite memory of the book coming out was going on Graham Norton's show in 1996 to promote it, and him giggling about the first recipe, which was basically 'MASH A BANANA'. They had a laugh about that being so obvious, but agreed that it was reassuring for new mums who might be nervous about what was best for their baby to know that something as simple as a mashed banana was a great idea and, most importantly, that it was enough.

The book I was using was going a little further, and we were adding ground cinnamon, peanut butter, cumin and even quinoa to Billie's meals. My dad said he didn't know what quinoa was until he was in his thirties – when he was a teenager, even cheese was exotic. Times were definitely changing. More ingredients are now a lot easier to get in supermarkets, and I wanted Billie to try everything. I'm quite fussy, and I *hate* that I'm like that. I remember being at a friend's house when I was around five or six, and not being allowed to leave the table until I'd eaten all my food. It was a pasta dish with sweetcorn in it, which I'd picked out, but I had to eat it before I could go and play. I'm ninety per cent sure this is why I hate sweetcorn to this day and why I was also giving Billie little bits of food, to get her used to eating with her hands, because this apparently makes babies less fussy.

One thing I was adamant about when it came to weaning was that I wouldn't worry about the mess. I didn't care at all how grubby Billie got, but no one really speaks about how grubby you and your house get. I made the mistake early on of giving her a whole bowl of food, which she threw everywhere. Suction bowls and plates were a new thing that my granny and mum couldn't get over. Billie had some strength on her though, so I had to still watch out . . .

We started with one 'meal' a day at 5 p.m., but in hindsight I wish I'd started doing it mid-morning, around 11 a.m. It was a little bit chaotic in the evening, as Steve likes to lay out all the things in the kitchen that he's going to use for dinner, so when I used the pot he wanted, it all got a bit complicated. Who wants to wash up before making dinner?! Our kitchen was tiny, which didn't help, and was another reason why we really needed to move house. Weaning is also the time you're introducing and on the lookout for allergens, and if I'd given Billie something like peanut butter for the first time earlier in the day, I would have had more chance of noticing a slower reaction.

A few weeks after trying various veggies for the first time, we were off to Scotland again. This time we were flying in a wee plane up to Dundee. I think it's the smallest airport I've been to, and my mum knew all the staff by name from when she commuted to London through it when I was at school. She used to fly down on a Sunday, do Monday and Tuesday's shows live, and then record the rest of the week on Tuesday before flying back up. Eventually, she had to do all the shows live, apart from Friday's, so she'd record that one on Thursday and fly back up then.

I didn't make a big deal of the flight because Billie was such an angel on the first one, but that was when she was eight weeks old. I thought I had been so clever ordering formula and nappies to pick up at the airport, but, of course, I'd read the order confirmation wrong – I was supposed to have picked them up 'landside', before security. I assumed the whole point of click-and-collect was that it would be after you've gone through all the liquid faff. Mistakes like this normally would just make me feel a bit silly, but anything to do with Billie made me spiral a bit. I would think, *If I can't get this simple thing right, then should I really be in charge of her? How am I supposed to be the one feeding and looking after her if I can't do this?* I'm so lucky I was with my parents and Steve when this happened, as they could help find a solution and tell me it wasn't the end of the world.

Now that Billie was six months old, we decided that her bottle at bedtime would be formula. I needed a break from breastfeeding, physically and mentally. It also meant that my mum or Steve could do the whole thing without me having to be there. Steve could have that time at night instead of clearing up the chaos after bathtime, which I would now do. We got so excited thinking about going out for dinner when we were in Scotland too, because my parents were coming with us and could look after Billie. Just the two of us having a meal together hadn't happened in half a year.

The flight was at 6 p.m., which was normally when Billie's bedtime routine started, and I think she got very confused as to why she wasn't in her bubble bath. It was also a propeller plane, so the noise and bright lights at that time of the evening didn't help. She was crying for the majority of the flight, and so was I. I had tried feeding her, changing her, cuddling her, but nothing was working. I was already on the brink of tears from messing up the nappies and formula order, so this on top was just a perfect storm. My mum took over and walked her up and down the aisle before she finally settled. I then got even more upset, because I wasn't able to soothe her, but also because I hadn't asked my mum earlier, when she was right there. I've never really liked asking for help, but now it was essential. You can't feel like a burden, and if someone is offering help, you should take it. Your pride isn't important, your baby is.

Once we'd landed, Steve was saying we'd need to wait for the bags and we should try to get Billie to sleep in the taxi, but he had never experienced Dundee airport before. As soon as you get off the plane and walk to the 'terminal', your bags are there on a conveyor belt that's just slightly bigger than one you'd get at the supermarket for your big shop.

In my head, I thought maybe she'd sleep all right after the trauma of getting there, but I was yet again proven wrong. I should have known by now that if you think something's going to go a certain way with a baby, it won't. What I was finding, though, is that it all did work out in the end.

I still hadn't got used to travelling and breastfeeding. I remember messaging my midwife about it. We were planning on going to my mum and dad's place an hour's drive away, and I couldn't understand how all the milk I had expressed would be OK on the journey. She told me to get a cooler bag with some of those freezer packs, and then put the milk in the fridge as soon as I got there. Fresh breastmilk can be transported within twenty-four hours of pumping, provided it stays at the same temperature, but I had milk that was maybe a day or two old, so I didn't know if this was the same thing (it can be kept in the fridge for up to four days). This all sounds completely logical now, but I was too terrified I was going to mess it all up. I've gone through some of the messages I sent the midwife, and thank God she was so kind to me. I was sending her videos of Billie sleeping next to me, asking her if the noises she was making were normal. Billie would do this weird strain as if she was doing a poo, but then her eyes would be closed, so I'd have no idea if she was unhappy and wanted changing or if she was actually sleeping and maybe having a weird dream. I sent the antenatal group mums, my mum and Steve's mum videos when she did this, who all either had a giggle with me or said it was totally normal. My support system in action!

I think Billie woke up five times that night, but she was in with us and went back to sleep really quickly. I would just whip a boob out while lying on my side, she'd have a quick feed, and that would be that. I was definitely still sleep-deprived, but I kept thinking how lucky I was that she went back to sleep right after and didn't cry too much.

She never cried enough for Steve to wake up, and it wasn't like he could feed her if he did wake up. At home, we were still sleeping in separate rooms. (I think it was more for my snoring rather than the mini sleep-thief.)

I felt totally fine leaving Billie with my parents on this trip so Steve and I could have a date night. My mum knew the drill, and I had also sent her the bedtime routine with bullet points. I did get one picture around the time she normally went to sleep of Billie in bed with my dad, and he didn't know that if you zoomed in on the mirror behind, I could see they were watching Dancing Fruit on YouTube. He'd never heard of it until a few weeks before, and I think he was more fixated than Billie. Dad and I had gone out for lunch together, and when Billie kicked off, the lovely woman that worked there gave us the remote for the TV and said to put on whatever we wanted. Billie never really watched TV and still doesn't, but watching Dancing Fruit with her grandad dancing along was pure magic. Steve and I were loosely following the rule of no screen time until she was two. She could watch TV if it was on for a tiny bit, but I didn't want her to be looking at our phones or the dreaded iPad. Steve always joked that the minute she turned two, she was getting one so we could go out for dinner and actually eat together! I didn't want her to be reliant on a screen for good behaviour. I sent a message back to them saying that I could see a pineapple with sunglasses doing somersaults in the background, and a few minutes later my dad sent me a picture of Billie and my mum both snoring and an apology.

My mum told me that, when I was really little, she was so scared about picking me up and making sure I was safe, but my dad would pick me up with one hand, and he was the one that shoved me into the bath for the first time. It was completely different with Billie. He either did everything so carefully or didn't do it at all, just in case something happened. I always thought I got my anxiety from my mum, but it was hiding all along in my dad.

I really noticed it that weekend. He was desperate to go swimming with Billie, and the hotel had an indoor pool. Like Billie, I was in the pool swimming before moving around on land, crawling or walking. My mum couldn't take me to classes because of the timings, so Dad took me to the Windsor baths. It wasn't organised swimming, so God knows what he was teaching me, but it worked and I loved the water. I was a total water baby and loved holding on to my heels and bobbing about like a little cork. I used to always be starving after being in the pool, and we'd either get a 'shivery bite'[†] of chips or go to Wimpy for a burger. They used to do a pudding of a doughnut with a scoop of ice cream in the middle, smothered with chocolate sauce. It wasn't such a relaxing experience watching Dad and Billie in the pool though. I stayed on the ledge taking pictures and videos of them, and all you could hear was my dad saying 'Is she too cold?' 'Is she doing a poo?' 'I think she's had enough now, she looks a wee bit tired', which was after about ten minutes. There was no trip to the football this time, but after all the hiccups at the beginning, it was so good to be up in Scotland and

---

† 'Shivery bite' is Scottish for a snack or something to eat to warm you up (stop shivering) typically after a dook (swim) in the sea.

Do What Works For You

get a fudge doughnut from Fisher and Donaldson (if you know, you know).

Once we got home, I took Billie to her first osteopath appointment to try to make sense of her hiccups, which came out of nowhere. Just as we were pulling up, the taxi driver said one of the most beautiful things I'd ever heard: 'Never don't pick them up, because one day they'll be picking you up.' After explaining to the receptionist why I was crying, we were then set for Billie's appointment. She had managed to stay asleep even while we were disembarking from the cab, so I had no idea how this was going to pan out. The only way to describe the osteopath was as a more masculine-looking Enrique Iglesias, if that's even possible. He was gorgeous – and I was in leggings with avocado smeared all over them from God knows what day and a massive oversized jumper that had paint marks on it. I couldn't have told you when I'd last washed my hair if my life had depended on it. He said it was normal for Billie to be sleeping for the appointment, and we wouldn't wake her up; he just said to pop her on the bed, and if she wakes up she wakes up. Billie still wasn't rolling or crawling at this point, but it wasn't something I was hugely worried about. Some of my friends' babies from the antenatal course had started, and they then couldn't take their eyes off them, so as much as I wanted her to develop, I was enjoying the fact that I could have a shower while she played with a toy lying on her play mat in the bathroom. Enrique said there was some tension in her abdomen, and he had released it. I didn't really understand how, but a few days passed and there were no more hiccups. I felt awful that I hadn't done this sooner. But I felt better once I had spoken to my parents about it, who said that baby osteopaths were never even on their radar when I was little. Granny had never heard that they even existed.

At this point, we were on two meals a day, one at 11 a.m. and another at 5 p.m. I'd bought more spoons, bowls and bibs, so I wasn't having to constantly wash the same ones. The admin of babies is never-ending. I thought it would get a bit easier in terms of the amount of stuff she would need now she was getting a bit older, but I'd gone from getting her more clothes because of milk sick to now getting her more clothes for a change after every meal. I knew there would be mess – but wow! People were not joking when they said babies get their food everywhere. The worst one so far was a puree of strawberries, spinach and butter beans. The red of the strawberries mixed with the green of the spinach to make a lovely deep brown colour. Billie ended up with it in her hair, in my hair, in her ears, splattered on the walls. I wish I'd bought her a high chair in brown rather than pink.

My mum told me I was really good at trying new foods as a baby . . . and was just as messy. There is a wonderful picture of us having a meal in Caffe Uno (RIP), me eating spaghetti bolognese with my hands at around four years old. No wonder my granny was appalled when we went out to eat.

With the weaning picking up now, I was also experiencing change. Charlie and Jo both told me that their hair fell out after having their babies, and that I shouldn't worry if I was washing my hair in the shower and clumps started to come out. I was prepared, but at first I really thought I had got away with it. I had started to clock a tiny fringe growing all around my hairline, but had seen women online who had it way worse. Hormones are wild. If I looked closely at my scalp, it looked like I was going bald. I was combing it over a bit so I didn't have to look at it, but apparently hair loss at six months postpartum is common, and normally kicks off around three to four months postpartum. I'd always had quite thick hair, which I get from my dad's side. Steve had to buy a few bottles of drain unblocker because my hair kept clumping in the drain and turning our shower into a mini bath. I tried to see the good side of it and told him it was like a free foot soak now and again . . . Mum and Granny said they never noticed their hair falling out, but that it was also something that was never spoken about, so they weren't sure if their friends or people they knew went through it.

I think my generation of new mums and those that come after us have incredibly different ways of communicating. You can find your people in your close friends who are experiencing similar life events to you, in fellow new mums you meet at baby groups, and also online. We have easy access to way more knowledge than those in my mum's generation, but sometimes this overload of information can be quite detrimental. I do think sometimes if social media didn't exist, or at least had more regulations about what you can post, that new mums wouldn't feel so overwhelmed with information they don't really need to know. When I asked my granny and Great-Aunt Josephine about 'baby blues', they had no idea what I was on about, because they'd never heard about it. I actually think this is a term we need to be so careful using now, as it can sounds dismissive, and might make women reluctant to tell their doctor how they are actually feeling. It was said to me by a few people before I started seeing my nurse for regular check-ins, and it made me think, 'Maybe that's *all* it is?' Luckily, I didn't listen, and I asked for more help. The next step for me was either group therapy sessions with other mums or Cognitive Behavioural Therapy (often shortened to CBT). I didn't like the idea of being so open and vulnerable with a bunch of people I didn't know, but the upside would have been meeting more mums and maybe becoming friends with people who understood how I was actually feeling. I wasn't as sad anymore by this point, but the worrying was sometimes overbearing. I was also still incredibly irritable. I decided to give CBT a go, and because I was already in the system, I got scheduled for weekly hourly appointments in the following days. The help I received was unbelievable, and something I wish more women had such quick access to.

These days, if women are feeling anxious or depressed, it's likely they know someone who has been through it – and that's because we talk about it. Maybe the women in my family, even before my granny, were struggling, but they didn't feel they could share they were feeling that way because all they were told was to 'just get on with it'.

It really feels like I've experienced a different world in becoming a mum, and not all of it is so positive. My generation is one in which your worth is closely linked to your productivity. All my granny had to think about was her babies and that was it, whereas my mum was also thinking about her mortgage, like I am. I love the fact that becoming a mother is no longer seen as the ultimate thing to do for a woman, or the only thing that should be given importance in our lives, but it also shouldn't be taken for granted. Becoming a parent is incredible – and extremely difficult. In a baby's first year, you're everything to them – you're their entertainer, private chef, cleaner, and, as much help as you do get, it does fall to you as the parent to know what to do. Even when they're sleeping, you're never off, just on standby. It's no wonder new mothers feel such burnout. You need to have a successful career, a thriving marriage, a bikini bod, a gorgeously clean home, and be the best friend you can be. Who can do all of that? Getting through each day and figuring out the next step is a huge achievement. Anything else is just a bonus.

11

~~'You'll make a rod for your own back'~~
Let the Baby Lead You

The hardest part for me at this stage of weaning was still breastfeeding. Billie was having more solids so didn't need to feed as much from me, but I was still producing the same amount of milk. I wasn't ready to stop, but I needed to get to grips with what to do now. I always said the minute Billie got teeth, I'd be done. At this time, she just had one bottom one, but another one next to it was just ready to pop out. Every Wednesday, the nearest community centre to us had their open morning for health visitors to weigh babies and check up on them. You didn't need an appointment, and at this one, the health visitor was a woman I'd not met before.

Billie weighed a perfect 9.6 kilos. Billie had her dummy in, and the health visitor said, 'You'll want to get rid of that by time she's one.' There were a few mums in my antenatal group who had already weaned their babies off their dummies, but it made Billie happy, and I didn't want to just take it off her to make myself feel like I'd achieved something. It soothed her immediately, and while there were occasions she was so tired she would just pass out, most of the time, especially at bedtime, it would be the last step to get her to drift off. My mum told me that I had a three-dummy routine until I was two – I'd sleep with one in my mouth and one in each hand. Billie, like me, didn't need them during the day, and if she did kick off I could give her one and she'd be as happy as a clam. I also got her matching dummy clips in pink, purple and cream so I could make sure they'd go with her wee outfits. One thing my mum didn't have for me was a dummy box, where I kept Billie's spare one. You can now even get boxes that sterilise them on the go. By far my favourite dummy gadget, though, was her glow-in-the-dark ones. I went from having three in her cot for emergency wake-ups in the night to just needing one.

This comment from the health visitor felt like a real intrusion about the decisions Steve and I were making about our own family. When it comes from someone in the health industry, it can make you question everything you're doing. They are the experts, yes, and they have such specialised knowledge, but this didn't feel like a suggestion and wasn't something that she expanded on, explaining why the age of one was best for getting rid of a dummy. It felt like a personal belief. The health visitor then did the one thing that annoys me more than anything else. I swear every mum has experienced this this – it's when people talk to you through your baby. I asked her about the fact that I was not breastfeeding as much because Billie was on solids, and her response was to look directly at Billie and act as if she was Billie's voice, saying: 'Mummy, I don't want you to stop feeding me.' I didn't even bother to correct her and say I hadn't meant that I wanted to stop breastfeeding. I don't know if she had misheard me, or was genuinely trying to help, but it didn't land well at all. I decided that instead of getting any information from her on the topic, I would go back to my mum, granny and friends.

Stopping breastfeeding wasn't too bad at all for my mum. I was already sleeping more during the night, and both of us just mutually decided to taper off (without me actually saying anything, obviously, as I was too wee).

At around eight and a half months, I moved Billie on to three meals a day. She absolutely loved her grub and was getting along with it all so well. I always put out bits of food she could grab along with her puree, and I ate it too, which meant she finally got the hang of it. I could give her a piece of toast the size of a finger, and she'd suck at it until it disappeared. I was still really scared of her choking, but I'd started to feel a lot calmer the more she ate. I was never giving her anything she could choke on, as everything was so finely chopped up, and she was also really good at spitting things up. I'd made a meal plan of everything she was going to have so I could make a shopping list and not just use one bit of broccoli and throw the rest out if it went funny. The one thing people don't talk enough about with weaning is food waste. The amount of things that either ended up on the floor or in the bin because she didn't want them was a bit heart-wrenching. I was just getting over my back pain from breastfeeding, and now there was a whole new kind of pain from constantly bending over to clean the floor!

Someone who was enjoying the mess was our dog, Ruby. Whenever I made Billie anything, I had to look up if it was dog-friendly, and it surprised me to learn that avocado can be harmful to some dogs.

Ruby really used to be the baby of the family. She has her own wardrobe, that includes a pearl collar (fake pearls, just to make it clear), and harnesses and collars that matched for her walks. She even has an Instagram account, although, to my shame, I've only posted about five pictures on it since Billie was born. Ruby was the one thing that tipped me over the edge sometimes when I was so overstimulated. She's always one to be involved and loves being at your feet, but when you're carrying a screaming and hungry baby, it became a bit much. Having said that, she did provide a very useful vacuum cleaner service when Billie was in the stage of throwing her food everywhere! I also kept thinking about how sweet it was that Billie would be growing up with a dog (who is, of course, obsessed with her because of all the food throwing).

In terms of feeding and solids, Billie was now having her morning milk, then breakfast, another feed if needed or wanted before a nap, lunch, a feed if needed or wanted, dinner, a feed again if needed or wanted, then her bottle of formula with her bedtime routine. I would always offer her a boob, but if she'd had a lot of food, the feeding would be really short. Having this structure really helped me, and I felt like a weight had been lifted off my shoulders. She was still not sleeping through the night, but she was definitely sleeping longer stints. We'd gone from five wake-ups to about three instead.

Let the Baby Lead You

Away from the baby milestones, we were finally moving house. Our offer had been accepted in October, and by now it was April. It would be another month until we were actually out of London. We got a huge email from our lawyer on a Friday morning with about eleven forms to fill in, and Steve had asked me if I'd done them all by Friday afternoon! When I had a look through them all that night, I said to Steve there was no way I could do it on my own now Billie was around, so I needed his help. I honestly don't think he thought it was a big deal, but I also didn't really trust myself with any kind of form now that 'baby brain' had taken over. I was still struggling with dates and times.

My mum said she experienced the same after having me, and also did the classics like leaving keys in the fridge and walking into rooms and immediately forgetting why she had gone in there. She said, and I agree, that it's down to trying to do too many things at the same time on zero sleep. My mum's big issue with baby brain was packing my nappy bag for a walk and then constantly leaving it at the door. Granny doesn't remember having baby brain, I think because women were just expected to get on with it and to not expect any help, especially from their husbands.

Baby brain isn't just a myth; a study into the changes that happen with your hormones and brain after birth was released in 2017.[*] The results showed that the mother's brain goes through the greatest structural change that any human goes through. The hormone oestrogen is involved in

---

* https://pubmed.ncbi.nlm.nih.gov/27991897/

the structural changes in the third trimester, which makes new mothers' brains adaptable, flexible and primed to learn quickly and figure things out. The study showed that pregnancy confers long-lasting changes in a woman's brain.

This doesn't happen with dads. I always think I'm letting Steve down when the brain fog comes into play. He must think I'm mad and not the person I was when we started dating, but it's quite reassuring that so many others experience the same thing. Whenever I wanted to kill Steve (and the feeling was probably mutual), I would always remind myself that we were both coping with huge life changes. I didn't want to nag him, but it was hard. I also didn't want to have a go at him for not doing things my way. There have been a few times where I've had to keep quiet and let him figure something out for himself, and there have also been times when I've said something, like, 'Don't put her in the shower after swimming because she hates it,' and he'll do it anyway. If I wanted to go to a pilates class or get my nails done, especially when it was a mealtime, I would play out a scenario in my head that he wouldn't want to help and instead he'd be busy running or wanting to go to the gym. I would get agitated and not bother asking him, which would then make me even more agitated because I hadn't taken any time for myself.

A 2021 study[†] found that 20 per cent of new parents split up in the first year of their baby's life. I couldn't wrap my head around that – that a baby that was made through love was ultimately breaking people apart – until we went

---

† https://psycnet.apa.org/fulltext/2022-16081-001.html

through it. Steve and I were still in the roommate phase, but there were little glimmers of hope that we still liked each other. We were sleeping and essentially living in separate rooms, though. His stuff was moved out of our room so he could get ready for the day without coming in early, in case Billie was sleeping (I could probably count how many times that happened). Before Billie, we would always get into bed together and talk about our days and how we were feeling, and not having that check-in meant we didn't really give time to each other. We weren't really talking. All our conversations were either about plans for dinner, who needed the car when, and checking our calendars to see when either of us could leave the house.

I had a lot of compassion that he was potentially feeling like a spare part in those early days. Instead of getting annoyed at him for not stepping in or giving up when Billie was crying and just saying, 'She just wants you,' I could see how sad he was. At the same time, I felt angry about how my life had completely changed and there was so much pressure on me, but Steve was still getting to go to the gym, going to work, talking to people who didn't have kids. Something I wish we had done, with hindsight, is talk more when I was pregnant about how we would still show up for each other, and not get too grumpy and take things out on one another. My biggest trigger was how Steve did everything in terms of the housework, so I couldn't complain I wasn't getting help, but I wanted him to be more involved with Billie. I was desperate to hang the washing up for a change! At this point, we had had a baby, were planning our wedding, and were in the middle of moving house. My granny always says everything comes in threes, and we were doing the three biggest things you could do!

Before I got pregnant, I wanted to give being freelance a go, and then when I knew I was going to have a baby, I wanted it to work more than ever. I was so lucky to not have to go back to an office and have that hanging over my head. My mum said leaving for work when I was awake was horrendous. When I was tiny, I'd be up when she would be going to the studio, and she would then spend most of the journey there in tears. My dad would always tell her I'd be fine after a couple of minutes, but she would have that horrible, sick, guilty feeling in her stomach that she was neglecting me. She said that the guilt and being a working mum go hand in hand, and it never got any easier.

My mum had to leave me with my dad for a whole week when I was around fourteen months. She was filming a special segment for GMTV called 'In the Villa' in Marbella, and then in the afternoon there was a spin-off with a longer version that would go out. It was a bit like her own show, but set in Spain for the week! It was the early nineties, so nothing like FaceTime or Zoom existed. My mum called every day, but said it's never the same. A few months later, she had to work abroad again, but this time for two weeks to film a special on the *Queen Elizabeth 2* (QE2). She was travelling from Southampton to New York, and although it was so exciting and a great career opportunity, she said that she would rather not have gone. With my dad being a freelance cameraman, he was able to take that time off work when my mum wasn't there and, even though he had help with a nanny, my mum said he still looked slightly frazzled when she got home. He was definitely around way more than most dads were at that time in the nineties, which was so lucky for me. When I was a teenager, we got on each other's nerves, but he always made sure I had my tea, and I knew if I called him at 3 a.m., he would come and pick me up. This is something I didn't think about until I was older, but he looked out for my friends too. He once picked me and Alex up from a school trip where we weren't told we needed a packed lunch so hadn't eaten anything all day. He was absolutely furious and called up to speak to our teacher. To this day, Alex says, 'If I murdered someone tonight, I'd phone Steve Smith to help bury the body.'

Sian, our nanny, came to help with me in the weekday mornings when I was around six months old. She would come at around 6 a.m. and stay until my mum got back from work just after lunchtime. I loved her to bits and when she left to look after her own two new babies, Helen arrived. She became my first best friend, and she stayed with us until we moved up to Scotland when I finished primary school. I wish we could have taken her with us. If my mum had been working the way she was now, she would have just taken me with her on all the shoots. The bosses would probably even want babies there to boost the ratings!

I was going to take going away without Billie in baby steps. My friend Jo told me that the first time being away from her boy wasn't easy. She'd planned on going out for dinner with a few friends, and had not been able to engage in any conversation. Her brain was somewhere else completely, and she wanted to rush home. The first time I left Billie, she was only eight weeks, and didn't really know what was happening. She was sleeping most of the time and could take a bottle, so I had a pump with me in case I got engorged, but I was only away for a few hours and didn't need it. I fed her before I left, and it was the first time I'd driven by myself since having her – and the first time I actually had something to eat on my own too. She was barely keeping her eyes open for longer than a couple of hours at that stage, so she didn't really know I wasn't there. I also don't think my mum let go of her the entire time!

The second time was when Mum and I went to a wedding in Yorkshire for the weekend. A few days before, I had gone to visit Jane, the breastfeeding consultant, again. I was so looking forward to showing her how much we had come along and, specifically, how big Billie was now. I think I wanted some reassurance that if I was going to leave Billie for two nights, we both wouldn't forget how the whole breastfeeding thing worked. I also needed someone I trusted to say what to do when it came to pumping, and to help me make a plan. My boobs were huge because I wasn't feeding her as much. Jane made me feel so much better and I left realising how far we had come. The first time she was at the house, I was crying non-stop and had a full-blown meltdown when I thought I had given Billie blisters all around her mouth. Now, she was nearly 10 kilos, loving her grub and definitely weaning off me. When I told Jane I had exclusively breastfed for six months, she said, 'Wow.' My mum had said how amazing it was

Let the Baby Lead You

I was able to do it, but hearing it from Jane, who was a professional, unbiased source, made me feel like I'd climbed a mountain.

When I was away that weekend, it was the first time I had slept through the night since I was heavily pregnant. I pumped around the time I would normally feed Billie, put the milk in storage bags as if I was keeping it, and then popped it in the mini bar. I was too excited that I was going to actually sleep, and not used to it at all.

The morning of the wedding, I scooted off to Marks & Spencer to get a strapless bra, having no idea what size I needed now. I didn't want to get properly fitted yet because the size of my boobs was fluctuating so much depending on the amount of milk in them. I grabbed a couple and ended up with an E cup, which made me laugh. I had pumped that morning, but they were obviously still huge.

I'd actually bought a new dress for the wedding, and it was something I'd never thought of wearing before. It was baby pink with appliqué detail all over it. I loved wearing tight dresses in pregnancy, and I think it was the most confident I've ever felt with how I looked. Now I had gone up a dress size, and was a totally different shape. One thing I didn't ever want to do was complain about how I looked in front of Billie. It didn't matter as much at this point, as she was so small, but I remember being around ten and going shopping with my mum, who needed something to wear for an event. She refused to try anything that showed off the top of her arms, and I think that's why I don't like showing mine off now. This is something I'll be so conscious of with Billie. I've always hated my tummy and arms, but she will never know this (unless she reads this when she's older!).

At the wedding, a few people thought they were being funny by asking, 'Where's the baby?' I felt like replying, 'Believe it or not, there's another parent, so she's actually with her dad,' but I refrained. I was missing her so much, but I was also loving some time on my own, only having to think about what I was going to eat that day. I had to go off into the groom's room upstairs to pump. My mum came with me, and I got her to throw the milk down the sink. Months of trying to store it and then throwing it away actually made me want to cry. I was finally getting the hang of the whole pumping thing, but now it would just be when I wasn't with her. I'd managed to express some milk for Steve, but if Billie had formula now as well it would be fine, because she was already on a bottle a day anyway at bedtime. We were calling formula 'daddy milk', which Steve loved.

This was Steve's first time on his own with Billie, and although I'd roped his mum into being there too, he was in charge. I had left Post-it notes of all her recipes and little designs of all her routines. For example, her pre-bedtime routine involved dimming the lights and having quiet, calm play time, then getting all things set up for success, like laying out her nappy, a book and her dummy. We could try to get Billie used to not feeding from me to get back to sleep, at night. The first night, Steve was messaging me saying she wouldn't go back to sleep, and it was hell. I told him to use his mum, because she was there to support him, and would love Billie cuddles no matter what time of the night it was.

Let the Baby Lead You

He got around four hours of sleep in total and, honestly, I didn't feel bad at all. Billie got up once around 10ish, like she would for a feed with me, then went back to sleep until 4 a.m. and had a bottle with her granny. When we got home on Sunday afternoon, I could see how much more confident Steve was. We had all survived, and because he had got so much out of it, I didn't actually feel guilty about being away.

12

'It goes so fast...'

Love Watching Them Grow

I was still waiting for the time to go fast. You don't really realise it until you look back at photos of your baby from a few months before and see how much they have changed. Maybe this is why my mum and every mum with grown-up kids now says this to new mums. My mum has maybe ten pictures of me as a newborn, and I think I have 330 of Billie from week one. We were about to embark on a brand-new adventure that would probably require an entire new phone for storage of the amount of pictures and videos needed.

Moving house with a baby was less stressful than I thought it would be. This was all down to the fact that, as we were moving so close to my parents, we could use their house as a base – and my dad was on hand to help too. I've never seen him so happy as when he's with Billie. My dad's favourite thing is doing 'baby on the head', where he picks her up and just puts her on his head. He used to do it with me, and it used to just reset me if I was crying. It did the same with Billie.

MOTHER TO MOTHER

My mum was away filming in Norway for two weeks, so the next time I'd see her would be in the new house. I stayed at my parents' house with Billie, and the 'men' did all the logistics. Steve helped the movers load our lives from the flat into their van, sent me some pictures of how bare it looked, and that was it. I never got to say goodbye to it, and it was the end of an era – Billie's first home, and the place where we were living when we got engaged. We had a lot of firsts there, but I was also so ready to move on to the next stage of our lives.

Moving into our new home wasn't what I thought it would be like, but I was slowly learning that's what happens with any big event when there's a wee one involved. I had visions of us surrounded by boxes, eating pizza on the floor. Instead, I was on my own at my parents', and secretly quite happy about it! Steve went completely mad and unpacked all the boxes in one night. Meanwhile, Billie went to sleep around 7ish, and I washed my hair, did a face mask and used my mum's portable foot bath, all while watching *Below Deck* (after making myself beans on toast). The perfect first night!

When we got into the house the next day, it felt like it was all meant to be. We had space. Billie had a playroom and a garden. The one daunting thing was not knowing anyone, so I had to build my village all over again. I knew I had my parents close, but after about the fourth garden-centre lunch with my dad, I realised I needed to make some friends. I signed up for the same music class I used to do in Islington, and I was so nervous. I do sometimes think making friends is harder than meeting someone and dating, which I also hated. I sat down next to another mum who had a little girl, and we got chatting, As soon as I said I had just moved there, she said we should exchange numbers, and I put my name in her phone as 'Billie's Mum'. This was something I wasn't used to seeing myself described as, but seeing it in writing was so lovely.

After my granny and grandad had my mum, they also moved. They were living in the Gorbals, not a nice part of town, and in the late 1940s it was actually one of Europe's worst slums, with about 40,000 people living in tenement housing where conditions were appalling. It's mad to my mum now that it's been gentrified and people are choosing to live there. Granny remembered that when she left my mum outside in the back where they lived for some fresh air, some bams* threw grit at the pram and it was all over her gorgeous white knitted cardigan and wee face. Granny cried her eyes out and knew they had to move.

As we were nearing nine months, this was a time of beginnings and endings. Billie's sleep was still a struggle, but it had got so much better. The two nights I'd spent away from her, not breastfeeding her through the night, hadn't sparked a lasting change. The first night I got back, I was feeding her to sleep, and I felt so guilty in the morning, as I'd specifically used my time away to try and break the habit. I was too exhausted to go and make her a bottle when all I had to do was whip a boob out. Then I saw a mum on social media talking about how the only way she could get her two-year-old back to sleep in the middle

---

* A idiot; a foolish, annoying or disruptive person.

of the night was breastfeeding him. Seeing that filled me with dread, and I decided that we would switch out Billie's night-time feeds with formula. I felt so lucky she took the premade formula, so I had that on my bedside table with bottles ready for action. The longest she had gone without waking up was from 7 p.m. to 3 a.m., so I knew she didn't need feeding at 10 p.m. anymore. This was the first feed we 'dropped' and I thought it was going to be painful, but actually it was fine. She woke up around 10.30 p.m. and I cuddled her back to sleep. That long stint of sleep in the night was now on her own in her cot, and she was now fully in her own room in the new house, which was more of an adjustment for me than for her. I was so used to her being in bed with us. Steve had moved back into the room, and we'd folded up his sofa bed. She was in the middle, he would be sleeping soundly on his side as always, and I would be on my side in some sort of Quaver crisp position, making sure everyone else was comfortable.

I'd seen a post on social media where someone was saying if you rock your baby to sleep, expect to be doing it until they're twenty-one. Luckily, this person was taking the mick out of all the mumfluencers who say stuff like this. After all, if there's a habit and it works, why break it? I loved rocking Billie to sleep and having that time with her when she fell asleep in my arms. One thing I've still found myself doing is rocking in all scenarios without Billie. If I'm in the line for a coffee or waiting on the pilates instructor doing a demonstration, I'll just be there in my own wee world, swaying from side to side. I've seen other women do this, and assumed they must have a baby at home.

Speaking of trends, after talking to my mum and Great-Aunt Josephine about my decision to stop breastfeeding, I learnt they'd each had the exact same experience. They got to nine months like I did and then tapered off, solely by taking cues from their babies. I wasn't ready to go completely off our routine, so we kept some structure, but with things like this I wanted to be guided by Billie. This was a moment where I fully entered mum mode, something I'd never been completely sure would happen. Learning cues, knowing your baby's likes and dislikes – this *will* come. It won't be there during the early days as you're still learning, but in time, it will come!

I could tell Billie wasn't that fussed anymore with boobs and she was happy with a bottle. So happy she would almost do a little dance when she saw it in her room, all ready for her after her bath.

Thankfully, I never had anyone tell me that I couldn't or shouldn't feed Billie. My friends did, though, with people asking them 'When are you stopping breast feeding?' 'Is she feeding again?' or 'She really shouldn't be feeding to sleep.' As expected, I did get some looks for using a bottle, but I never felt uncomfortable. Like mum, I was really worried about Billie liking bottles more than me. Just as I had when I was a baby, Billie preferred breastfeeding, but would also give me a break and take a bottle. I remember my boobs leaking in a gym class when Billie was about five months, which I thought was down to the movement of running (which I hadn't done in over a year), but it was actually the time I normally fed her. Even though it's the most natural thing in the world, I still told the instructor I had a sore foot rather than saying I could feel milk coming out of my sports bra. It was the first time I had properly leaked in public after constantly thinking it might happen. I think it must have happened to every woman. I'd like to think that if I had another baby and this happened again I wouldn't care and would just say what was actually happening.

My mum also experienced this, but it was a bit more glamorous. She was standing in for Gloria Hunniford on her Radio 2 show for a week, about three months after I was born. Mum was wearing a maternity dress and interviewing the actor Michael Praed, who starred in the TV series *Robin Hood*, and was quite a heartthrob with very silly hair. (He had equally silly hair in *Dynasty*, but I'll let you do your own research.) Once he'd left the studio, Mum remembers looking down at her chest to see two enormous wet patches, and thought that he must have been too polite to say anything. Her contract hadn't been renewed at GMTV, so she was taking any work that was going. She'd even travelled back to Scotland to see her old bosses from STV and BBC Scotland, telling them she was essentially a taxi for hire. She had no maternity rights as a freelancer, and neither did my dad with his paternity leave, but he was having to look after me so was turning down work. Even if he hadn't been freelance, there wasn't such a thing as paternity leave thirty years ago. It did mean he was there and around to help, but he wasn't bringing in any money. Neither of them were. My mum had three months of not working, and that whole time, she didn't know when she would be making money again. I can't imagine the stress of that and having a newborn.

It's why I love seeing my mum with Billie now, because she's getting a chance to do it all over again, but without the stress – and with sleep! I caught my dad speaking to his friend about being a grandad when I don't think he knew I was listening. He was saying it was like doing it again, but with all the best parts. If we were staying at my parents', I would hand Billie over so I could get some sleep, and then I'd wake up a few hours later to notifications on my phone of them having breakfast with her.

Mum eventually went back to GMTV for two days a week for a mum-and-baby slot. The sponsorship deal specifically stated that she had to present that segment, and a few months later she had her own show, five days a week. The normal maternity leave now, thirty years later, freelance or not, is a year. The thought of going back to work when my mum did is crazy to me, because I was still deranged myself at that time. There is so much your body is still going through, and huge developments that you need to be there for, never mind how your hormones are still all over the place. I felt like I was just managing to string a sentence together – at nine months!

Having gone through mastitis and then shingles, I was desperate not to get it again. Rates of mastitis from breast-feeding in the UK and globally vary, but studies suggest it affects 30–33 per cent of women, often occurring in the first few weeks after birth, while 6–8 per cent of women may experience recurrent episodes of mastitis.[†] I could feel

---

† https://patient.info/doctor/history-examination/puerperal-mastitis

lumps in both of my boobs and I didn't want to pump, because that would just make them keep filling up, but I had to do something. I did give in one night when they were outrageously big, and filled four storage bags. I labelled the bags with the date and volume just by habit. If you had told me in the early days of feeding, or any time in the first six months, that I would be storing that amount, I wouldn't have believed it. I would have probably cried, too, when I realised I would have to throw it away.

I never knew my mum had mastitis until I had it – it's like she forgot, or had blocked that part of her early mum experiences out! Like me, she also tried the old wives' tale of putting cabbage leaves in the freezer, and again like me, it didn't really help. She said her boobs were red, angry and really painful, but she was still able to feed me. Her GP said I was thriving, just like Billie was with her gorgeous rolls, and Mum was producing 'gold top' (when milk was delivered door to door, gold top had a lot of cream in it). Mum had a hand pump that she hated using, and I think what was more horrible for her was having to do it away from me when she was working, normally sitting in a loo. She had no way to store the milk, so she had to flush it.

My two friends from antenatal class were in the same situation as me. They weren't stopping breastfeeding entirely like I was, but decided not to do it as much now that their babies had started eating more solids. Ulrika had the problem of an oversupply, and Rhiannon had gone through mastitis, which then led to an abscess. Both had done hand-expressing and told me I should give it a go. It made me think about collecting colostrum when I was pregnant and that freaked me out, as I just didn't trust myself that I would be doing it the correct way. Their mutual tip was to be patient and even put a podcast on. Ulrika was told that Sudafed would help with the pain of engorgement, but it didn't work for her.

It took about four or five times to try with hand expressing before it actually worked. I considered giving up and just pumping for the rest of my life. The first time it worked for me was in the shower. I tried doing it over the sink, but seeing my reflection in the mirror put me off! You have to do what makes you feel comfortable and not just go along with what people say they do. I had to cup and squeeze my boob to the nipple – and I had never seen the milk come out like this. There was always Billie there, or if she had come off the latch at any point it would spurt everywhere. Sometimes back in her face . . . (My friend was once breastfeeding and their baby fell asleep, came off and then milk splashed all over her wall. If you've ever had a Lucozade Sport from that very particular bottle, you'll know what I mean).

There was only one night when I kept waking up what felt like every half-hour in so much pain. Billie was having the night of her life, sleeping soundly with her white-noise machine and smelling of her baby coconut sleep oil, in a very soft sleeping bag with her cuddly toy. It got to 1 a.m. and I knew I had to do something. I didn't have the energy to get in the shower, so it was time for me to hand-express over the sink. It didn't take long before it started, this time just dripping out and not being as aggressive as it had been. Perfect timing, as Billie woke up crying. Steve put her in bed and tried to get her back to sleep, but I think she had a superpower smell that milk was in the air. Steve tried to cuddle her to sleep, so once I had got most of the huge lumps in my boobs down and didn't feel so swollen, I hopped into bed and she calmed down almost immediately. I loved it so much that she needed me and she liked me.

This was something I'd been terrified of when I was pregnant. I remember crying to Steve about not bonding with our unborn baby; I wasn't worried about me loving her, but her loving me. A lot of mums and dads don't have that immediate bond with their children when they're born, and then think that something is wrong with them. This is completely normal, and it's so important to not compare yourself to others, especially with what you see online. How and when that bond develops can be totally different. My mum felt an instant connection with me, but my dad didn't until he got me home from the hospital, which was probably when he had me on his own for the first time.

I don't know when my last breastfeed was. The last feed in our schedule that I dropped was the first one when she woke up. I had bought myself booby packs that looked like flower petals, where your nipple is at the centre of the flower, popping out. They could be left in the freezer for a few hours before you used them, and could also be heated up in the microwave. I had midwives telling me to use the cold setting for after a feed, and the hot one for before a feed to help stimulate the milk. I then had a doctor tell me to use heat on them to help stop feeding, so the conflicting advice never ends, but now I had the confidence to ignore it. I felt, for me, that cooling them down after I had done a bit of hand-expressing helped. Breastfeeding really is a superpower, but I feel like I can only say that now I'm not doing it anymore.

One thing I was really proud of was Billie's baby book. We got it as a gift from my mum's brother when I was pregnant, and I started to fill it out with all the bump bits and scans. The nurses said you had to pay for the ultrasound scans to take them home, but she slid them in my bag and said not to tell anyone. My parents still have one of me when my mum was pregnant. It's tiny. My dad framed it and it still sits above his computer. I found the baby book my mum had for me around seven years ago, when my mum and dad left Scotland again for England. I was so excited to look through it, but it was blank. I think that's maybe why I've gone a bit mad with Billie's and have filled every single page to the brim. It barely closes and it goes up until she's five. Steve's mum gave me her Mothercare one for Steve right after we told them we were going to have a baby. He had the same blond ringlets I did – and I don't know that from just pictures, as she sellotaped some of his hair in it too! If I ever think I've taken it too far with cherishing memories with Billie in these early days, I think of that.

Our neighbour gifted us the most beautiful Peter Rabbit-themed milestone cards when Billie was born. My parents had decorated my nursery with Peter Rabbit and I remember having Jemima Puddle-Duck, Benjamin Bunny, Flopsy, Mopsy and Cotton-tail scattered all over the wallpaper.

Mrs Tiggy-Winkle was my favourite. When I was around five, there was a hedgehog in our garden, so I set up a Mrs Tiggy-Winkle rescue centre made out of a cardboard box. I tried to take a picture of Billie with the cards on the given day she turned a week, a month or four months old, but I think I only managed it with the first one. I wasn't going to beat myself up if I took it a day or even five days after I was supposed to. The only person who would know was me. Baby brain did strike again when Steve's mum messaged me to say she had zoomed in on the date in one of these pictures and I was a whole year out . . .

With the move, I had missed doing the milestone 'nine months in, nine months out' pictures. This is one of my least-favourite phrases, as I felt it was more like a deadline for mums. Before I had Billie, I saw it as a cute way of seeing how far mums had come, and how wild it was that the tiny bump they'd once had was now a baby, nearly a year old. Now, I see it quite negatively, as so many people judge the way a new mum looks at this point. Social media comments flood in on how flat your tummy looks, and whether you've managed to bounce back. I looked about five months pregnant at nine months out, and I couldn't post a picture of myself dressed up because none of my clothes fit me, and I couldn't find any new ones I liked.

My own milestone was finally deciding to pack all my nursing bras away and get a fitting. I used to think that at bra fittings, you'd have to get your boobs completely out, and when I was a teenager I was terrified that would be the case. I expected to have gone up a whole chest size,

Love Watching Them Grow

but had no idea when it came to the cup. Now I wasn't pregnant and had stopped breastfeeding, I had gone from a 32DD to a 34D. It was quiet when I went and the woman was so lovely. I always find it to be wee old ladies that do the fittings, usually with fringes and glasses. She put me in the bigger changing room so I could fit Billie and the pram in, and then gave me a bra to try on. Once I was ready, she wrapped a measuring tape around me, and then came back with six bras for me to try on. A bit excessive, but it was a big day.

I had a minute when I was looking at my reflection in the changing room. I never understand why every single mirror makes you look like a total stranger. (Also, whenever I go to try anything on, I immediately need a wee.) I'd never had stretchmarks anywhere when I was pregnant, but now I had these purple-going-silver stripes all over my boobs from breastfeeding. I didn't have a waist anymore and my skin was so dull-looking. It's a bit controversial, but I think it's OK to have a big cry now and again to do with how you look and how your body has changed. My first big cry was a few days after Billie's birth. I was still in my disposable pants, hair not washed for days, and my belly had gone down, but not as much as I thought it should have at that point. The uterus usually takes six to eight weeks to shrink, but I didn't know that at the time. I caught a glimpse of myself in my bathroom mirror and cried uncontrollably for about ten minutes, which is a long time. My cry in the Markies changing room was tiny compared to that, but I was still overwhelmed by everything that had changed. Breastfeeding had stopped, my boobs had stopped fluctuating in size and my body was now settling into itself again. For my mum, it didn't take her long to heal physically, but it took far longer to get her confidence back. She went back to work when I was six months old, and luckily she could get hair and make-up done at the studio! She said it took about a year to feel like herself again. Like me, she was more concerned about being healthy, rather than being slimmer. I wanted to be fit and strong so I could carry Billie, not so that I could fit into my old clothes.

I left with two new very exciting basic bras, one black and one tan, and a little two-piece Peter Rabbit outfit for Billie. I couldn't resist – clothes for her were on the same floor! I didn't get any new clothes for the upcoming holiday to Spain I had planned with Jo (who had just moved back home from Singapore), Charlie and their little ones. We had decided to go away on a girls' trip with our bubs (and Jo's son), and it was something I'd been so looking forward to. When we had all been away together a couple of years before, Charlie's baby girl had stood up for the first time on her own and walked (with some help), so the thought of us being there now with Billie too was so exciting.

They were flying from Bristol and I was going from Heathrow, so I would be travelling solo with Billie. I was lucky because she still wasn't crawling and was very happy just sitting looking at everyone else but me. One thing I hadn't considered was how I was going to carry everything on my own. I also couldn't really do the ordering of nappies or formula at the airport, because then I'd need another arm. I had two suitcases, the car seat and the pram folded up on the trolley, then Billie in the carrier on me and a backpack filled exclusively with her things. My plan was to still be breastfeeding at this point so I could easily feed her and calm her down on the plane if she kicked off. I had spoken to Jane about this, and she said that if Billie took a bottle and was food-motivated, I could distract her that way. If the worst came to the worst, I could get a boob out. She said that she was once on a long-haul flight with her son, who was so unhappy she started breastfeeding him. She wasn't sure if any milk was coming out, but it worked. Her husband even looked over and said, 'I thought you'd stopped that months ago?'

Billie was perfect on the flight and so was everyone around us, apart from the poor man who sat next to us. I said sorry to him when he sat down, and I think I told him she was a really good baby about five times. She was desperate to make friends with him, but he was having none of it. Disembarking was slightly difficult, but I managed to put her in the carrier while I was still sitting down and then a really lovely older man got her pram down and said I'd done a 'stellar job', which nearly made me cry. Another reminder that if anyone ever asks if you need help, say yes. Also that if you see a mum doing a good job – or anything, actually – tell them they're amazing.

The girls were already there when I got to the villa and their babies were in bed. Once I'd got Billie down, we had drinks on the terrace and made a pact that this would be our ritual every night. The next five days were completely nuts. Jo's son was four and a half and

Charlie's daughter was two and a half. They were walking, running, eating, and I couldn't imagine Billie being like that one day.

I didn't realise it until we were there, but Billie was the easiest. Jo's son having to go to the water park one day was non-negotiable, and he also had to be in the pool most of the day, so Jo was a lifeguard the whole time and didn't really get much time to relax. Charlie's daughter was the opposite and was not a fan of the water, to the point of not even wanting a bath, so Charlie was inside most days watching *Peppa Pig*. Once we'd all individually done bedtime on our own, we would sit on the terrace and say the same thing at the end of each day: 'Why did we not bring a granny with us?' It was the first holiday we'd all been on when we were counting down the days until we flew home!

One of my favourite things was seeing Jo's son interacting with Billie. He wanted to feed her breakfast, pick the outfits she was going to wear and even help with changing her bum. He would always come with me to our room, which gave Jo five minutes of peace, and he'd get the nappy bag all ready for her dirty nappies. It was adorable and made me think about how much I'd love another baby, but then I'd have to go through pregnancy again, do the birth again and, worst of all, go through postpartum again. When Billie was a newborn and really giving Steve and I a hard time, he would always say the phrase 'one and done'. This would annoy me so much, because he knew I wanted more than one, and we were in the thick of it and in no position to be making any decisions. If anyone thinks about having another baby right after having one, they are mad. Lovely but, fundamentally, mad. Being an only child never bothered me at all, but I would just love to have a big family. I couldn't imagine having another baby and loving it as much as Billie at this moment, though! Would I love them the same or would the love I have for Billie be dwindled down to make room for the new one? How on earth would I be able to look after a newborn and also look after Billie? I was already over people asking me when we were having another baby the first time it happened. I'd like to think people would have the sense to not ask a woman when she plans on having kids, so asking when she plans to have another shouldn't be any different.

One morning we were having breakfast, and Jo's son asked me why Billie didn't have a penis. I wasn't sure what Jo was saying in terms of what body parts are called, so I told him that she had a front bottom instead. Luckily, Jo came up behind me and took over, telling him that Billie had a vagina – a word I didn't know until I learnt about it at secondary school. My mum never said anything like that to me, about what things were called, and she never had the whole period talk with me, either. She asked if I knew what all of that was when I found a tampon in her bag! It always stuck in my mind, and I decided that, if I ever had a girl, I would give her that chat, as uncomfortable as it would be for both of us.

The whole holiday was a glimpse of what was to come with Billie, and I was terrified. It taught me that when people had told me to cherish every moment, I now knew what they meant. Each phase was hard, but it was going to be a different type of hard. Which is really the theme of motherhood. I got chatting to two women when we were all waiting for our luggage at the airport. They had children in their twenties now and were telling me that they were at uni, going off into the world, and how worried they were. Another indication that you never really get a break . . .

This was definitely the case with tantrums. Jo's son was over that stage now, but Charlie's daughter was in the thick of it. Her being furious that Cheerios were round was something we could all see the funny side to, but when it came to every small decision being a huge to-do, I could see how much of a toll it was taking on Charlie. We had many a cuddle with our wine on the terrace after her daughter had gone down, and Charlie would burst into tears.

The holiday leaps were happening with Billie, who started to clap on day two. I had been waiting for this one, and I think her being around two older babies meant she wanted to show off a new skill. What I wasn't prepared for was being woken up at 3 a.m. to her clapping away, extremely happy with herself. On day four she slept through the night, so of course I tried to re-do everything the exact same way the following day, but that time she woke up in the night. It was just once now, and after a wee cuddle she was back in the land of nod. I felt very chuffed with myself that after that she was sleeping through, not in a cot but next to me in bed. She wasn't rolling yet, so I could leave her there with pillows around the bed just in case, but I really felt like we had turned a corner.

Love Watching Them Grow

We had done a full week of solo parenting between the three of us, with all different highs and lows. Charlie gave a great piece of advice me when I said I didn't know what I was going to be like when Billie kicked off and I couldn't do anything to calm her down. She said to ask myself if I could 'control the no'. It doesn't just work for their behaviour, but also stuff you can't change. Charlie's daughter used to get really bad travel sickness whenever she got in the car, so 'controlling the no' for her meant preparing for the scenario. You can't avoid going places and using the car, so sick bags and travel wristbands were tried and tested.

At the end of the holiday, we headed to the airport and made it past security where we had to split up because I was on a flight to Heathrow and they were going to Bristol. We all hugged, and the last words I said were how much I loved spending time with them and the babies . . . and then 'never again'. I didn't realise there was a group of older mums behind us that must have had kids or been grannies, because they all burst out laughing. Not at us, but with us!

The week we returned, Billie and I were going to London to go on Mum's show, and I decided to go in with her super early in the morning. I had a plan that I'd keep Billie in her sleep sack, transfer her into her car seat and she'd sleep on the way there. This didn't happen. As soon as she knows my mum is in the vicinity, a switch goes off in her brain alerting her that it's play time. I needed her to sleep a bit more, otherwise she was going to be very cranky on live TV, so the whole time we were in the car and in the dressing room, I was on edge. She did have a tiny nap that meant she missed the trailer for the show on *Good Morning Britain*, but it did mean she was awake and a total star on her granny's show. She was clapping, babbling away, laughing, and even stood up holding on to my mum's hands.

She was showing signs of wanting to walk by now, and I think just couldn't be bothered with crawling. Before we had moved out of London, I went on a mum date in a park that also had a 'stay and play' happening. Islington had areas where you could go for free with toys for the babies, and this one even had an 'expert' for the day who could answer questions about your baby. I say an expert in inverted commas, because this woman just told me Billie should be crawling by now, which I didn't find that helpful. Having textbooks telling you where babies should be at given ages is mad to me, because the people that write them then say every baby is different. There's no real 'textbook baby'. You just have to take the information you trust and which works for you. I said to myself what I said to my friend when her baby refused to walk, way before I'd even thought about having kids: 'They're not going to be bum-shuffling into their first job.' Billie was happy, and everyone could see that. My big worry was that there would be trolls after Billie was on the show saying I was a terrible mum because she wasn't on the move yet, but everything was really positive. I just had to let my anxiety ruin a lovely moment (again).

Everyone has their moments when they feel like the worst mother in the world, and mine came at around this time, when Billie fell for the second time. This time, she fell forwards onto the ground when I hadn't strapped her into her pram. I stupidly put her in and then put the changing bag underneath, and a split second later she was on the floor. It was horrendous. She cried with real tears, but after a cuddle, a dummy and strapping her back in to go to the pharmacy, she was fine. I rang the GP and they said to just get some arnica and keep an eye on her. By the time I got out of the park where it had happened, a little red mark had appeared on her head, and I couldn't bear it. I called my mum crying, and she told me it was going to be OK – and then Paul Mescal ran past me in his tiny little white Adidas running shorts. Two girls sitting on a bench were watching, and one asked the other if that was the guy from *Normal People.* I inserted myself into the conversation, saying, 'YES IT'S HIM, I'VE BEEN WAITING TO SEE HIM FOR MONTHS.' By the time we got home, the mark had almost gone. Babies are built for new parents making stupid mistakes, but it was still a wake-up call.

One day, my friend Ulrika and I were sitting on picnic blankets feeding the babies fruit when we saw a mum walk past pushing a pram with a bassinet, meaning her kid was still under six months. All we wanted to do was run over and tell her everything would be OK. Of course, she may well have been finding the whole experience of motherhood great, but now whenever I hear someone's pregnant or has just had a baby, I obviously feel so happy for them, but also so sorry for them. We were there with a picnic blanket, our babies sitting like real little humans eating real food, and I was actually wearing a dress. I wasn't covered in sick, I had washed my hair the previous day, and all I could think about was when was the last time this woman had slept. I wanted to say to her, as challenging and isolating as motherhood is, it gets better – it really does.

13

'Just you wait...'

It Gets Better and Better

The amount of times people said to 'just wait' until Billie crawled, because then I really wouldn't be able to do anything, was astounding. I already felt like I couldn't get anything done, so having this dark cloud hanging over me with what was to come actually took away from enjoying the stage I was in.

I started walking at fourteen months, so the fact that all Billie wanted to do was stand up, lean on anything in her eyeline, which was normally my leg, and do a wee dance up and down made sense! Out of nowhere, she then started to put one foot in front of the other, very *Fawlty Towers* style, with her legs getting really high up in the air before touching the ground. I think it was being in a new house, having more space and getting to use her baby walker, which she had inherited from my mum's brother, that did it.

We'd had a good run. Some of my friends' babies were crawling at six months, and one was up walking at nine. We didn't need to babyproof the house or get stair gates. Whenever I tried to get her to crawl, she just lay down on the ground as if she had given up on everything. I tried the trick of putting toys on the other side of her playmat, thinking she'd want to get to them, but she couldn't be arsed. Steve thinks it's because she was a big girl, so having to pick herself up would be hard. When I looked at the other babies moving about, they were a lot smaller.

My mum and Granny had a slight falling-out over how big I was. They were up in Scotland and I had on my famous tartan babygro – which Billie was in for her first Christmas – and my granny said to my mum, 'Oh hen, she's a wee bit plump.' Looking back at the photos, my mum said I did have a baw heid,* and she was right, but no one, not even her mum, was allowed to say anything remotely negative about me. I lost all the weight when I got my first cold and started moving more, but there is nothing quite like a chunky baby. Billie's thighs are a wonder of the world. She was properly eating with her hands by this time, sometimes very daintily, when she would pick up raspberries I'd halved, and other times not so, when she'd shove an entire pancake in her mouth.

I was struggling with rompers because they would fit her on the top part fine, but the elastic bits around her thighs were so tight they'd leave marks. Rompers were the cutest thing when she was up on her feet. She was walking a few steps, and I was very bored one day, so it was off to Clarks to get her some shoes. My logic was if we were out and she was kicking off because she wanted to get moving, if she had shoes on I wouldn't worry too

---

*Baw heid – a person with a large, round face.

much about her feet on the bare ground. I got my first shoes from Clarks, and all my school shoes, and it was very sweet having Billie get her feet measured in the same contraption I remembered. She was a size 4 and the woman in the shop said she had very wide feet. Naturally, I gave her the dirtiest look imaginable.

Billie still only had two teeth that had come through at this point, but she was chomping away on anything that came her way. When we were away, I gave her an ice cream on the beach for the first time, and she lost her mind. I got a Magnum, bit off all the chocolate around the sides, and then let her go wild. Her face lit up, and thank God Charlie was on hand to be a photographer, because I got the most amazing picture of her. I don't think she thought it would be that cold. At first her wee face screwed up, then the pure elation arrived, and soon she was squishing it with her fingers into her mouth, making a fabulous mess. My mum remembers giving me a pokey hat[†] for the first time from the ice cream van, back when a 99 was actually 99p. My mum was the same way I am with Billie, not caring how grubby I got. She wanted me to touch the food and feel the different textures, and she didn't worry about it being it all over my face and even in my hair.

I didn't like seeing babies having their faces wiped clean after every mouthful. No adult would want to be subjected to that sort of treatment when out for a meal. I found that Steve and my dad would worry about the mess whenever they fed her. Steve would even wear an apron when feeding

---

† Ice cream cone.

her so he didn't get covered, but I couldn't care less. I was already gross, so what's a bit of green stuff going to change? I never rush Billie with her food, and even though I want her to be done at some point, especially if it's dinner and we have to do bedtime, if you put yourself under pressure, it gets so stressful, and babies pick up on it. Things don't have to go to a strict time schedule every day, and that's OK. Women, and new mums especially, are under such pressure, and if you meticulously plan every second of the day with a baby, you're setting yourself up to feel like you've failed.

When we got home, I took Steve and Billie to the ice cream van so he too could experience Billie going mad. What was more hilarious was Ruby licking all the ice cream that was dripping down Billie's chest to her belly. She then had a bite of the end of the cone. I thought Billie would be upset, but she was too much in the zone to care. She was in a jumper and leggings that had to be taken off immediately and switched with a wee vest before we got in the car. Steve didn't freak out about the mess, and found the whole thing so lovely. I don't think I'd seen him that happy in a long time. When we found out we were having a girl, I said he would be getting his nails painted and have to pretend to be a princess at tea parties with all the stuffed toys. He said that would not be happening, but I knew then she had him wrapped around her finger. We just needed to make sure we had some nail-varnish remover in the house. My grandad once forgot and got some very strange looks after going to the pub in East Kilbride with hot pink, sparkly nails.

It Gets Better and Better

With all these tiny things that you take for granted, like getting an ice cream, it's as if you get to experience things again for the first time. When Ulrika and I took the babies to the aquarium in London, I was nearly in tears seeing Billie's little face watching the jellyfish. She was so entranced, watching them floating around, and when we saw the sea turtles it was so beautiful.

It can even happen with things as trivial as toothpaste. We were given a baby toothbrush when Billie was born, and Steve was keen to start using it. I have to admit I thought it was a bit silly, but we decided that if we started her young, it was a good habit for us all to be in. When I was a baby, my mum used to use her pinkie finger as a toothbrush, and covered it with Punch and Judy toothpaste that was bright pink and tasted like bubblegum. We had a bright yellow silicone finger puppet with a brush on the end for Billie, and she absolutely loved it. I think she loved the taste of the baby toothpaste – and so did Steve. The nostalgia got to him, and I did sneak him having a wee taste of it the first time we brushed her teeth. We had no idea when to introduce it into her routine, because sometimes she fell asleep having her bottle, so if we brushed her teeth then, we were worried it would wake her up and it might take ages to get her back to sleep.

Now I wasn't breastfeeding anymore, Steve and Billie could spend ages together without him having to worry about her being hungry. He could now technically spend all day with her, just the two of them. Our new routine now is that Fridays are my day to work, and we call them 'Daddy Fridays'. It wasn't long before I realised I had to leave the house to get work done, though. After a few hours of working at home, I'd give up. Steve always wanted to show me what she was doing, whether that was playing with a toy or walking, things I'd seen tons of times. The one time it did annoy me was when he shouted, 'She's done a poo,' implying that dealing with this was a two-person job. I'm not sure what he thinks I do when I'm on my own with her, but I had to keep telling myself that he wasn't used to doing it all the time. He's also genetically unable to multitask.

When you have a baby with someone, you see the best and worst parts of each other, and after nearly a year of doing this together, I think I've cracked how to know you've done it with the right person. The rage is real, and if you can get over being annoyed at them, and even hating them sometimes, and go back to the love, then it's right. You'll also feel so jealous of your partner at times, which adds to the rage. They can do whatever they want, any time. They'll never be able to understand what you've gone through, so as annoying as they will be, it's good to have that as a reminder. Women need other women to rant with. People who have been through it and get it. I'd actually felt so much better about our relationship after I'd had a good old rant about him to my friend who'd had a baby at around the same time. It became our thing: exchanging what stupid things our partners had said or done that week.

One day, the house was about to be full, as I'd gone to the airport to pick up Great-Granny, Great-Aunt Josephine and Uncle Graham. My dad had mysteriously vanished to Spain to play golf, and Steve was working, so I was the driver for the week. I found that with more people in the house, and Billie as the on-hand entertainer, I was able to get a lot done. I could also trust she wasn't in any danger because she wasn't moving on her own. That week, I made broccoli and cheesy tots, a pizza with a cauliflower base, and, for the first time, a meal all of us could eat, with some adjustments and a bit of admin. I decided to make a massive bowl of chilli con carne to feed us all, and did a separate one for Billie without salt. One thing I built up too much in my head was how complicated making food for her would be. Yes, you can get all these recipes bombarding you on social media saying to use organic buckwheat, but I found with snacks or muffins it was just a case of mixing stuff together and then baking it. After all, I wasn't going to be getting a famous Paul Hollywood handshake from Billie. Things not being perfect was OK. Billie had no idea, and she was very happy with any kind of snack, made with organic ingredients or not.

I took advantage of the help and went out on my own for an afternoon of maintenance. I would say pampering, but I got my eyebrows threaded, and that's the least relaxing thing anyone can do. A word of advice: if the woman doing the threading offers to do your moustache, say no. I have never felt pain like that in my life, and I've had a needle in my back for an epidural. I got a massage, too, and that was so lovely, because I think it was the first time I lay down on my front and my boobs weren't sore from being full of milk. I'd not spent that much time on my own since I was pregnant. I'd had maybe half an hour when the car needed petrol, and instead of just filling it up the next time we went out, I went out to have some me time. I even drove the long way home so I had even more time to myself. A real treat for five minutes – before the guilt set in that I had no reason for not being at home and not being with Billie. I took nothing for granted anymore when it came to simple things like getting my eyebrows or nails done, or going on a date night with Steve.

We'd planned to all go to the pub for lunch the next day, and on the way there we were all squashed in the car. Josephine was sitting in the back with Billie and, as we saw a mum pushing a pram on the pavement, she said she didn't like that the baby wasn't facing the mum. 'What if something blows in the baby's face and it chokes?' The 'what if' is something I thought I'd grow out of as Billie grew, but Josephine is nearly eighty years old and showed me that feeling never goes away. I know I'll be exactly like my mum was with me. When I used to go out in my teens and twenties, she would stay in the living room, sleeping on the sofa and waiting for me to come in.

Billie was going through a real growth spurt in her last month before turning one. She had finally started to crawl and, of course, when she did, I wasn't there. Steve had her playing on the sofa with all her toys, but the only thing she wanted was the TV control. He put it on one end of the sofa and, voilà, she was off. I immediately ordered some stair gates and babyproofing bits for the house. We'd had a good run of not needing to keep an eye on her every second, as some babies we knew were moving at 6 months.

Her next milestone was her first birthday. I'd been planning Billie's birthday party in my head for months. We were torn between the themes of the Hungry Caterpillar and party animals. She loved the book, and would giggle whenever her dad read her the page when the caterpillar turned into a beautiful butterfly, but when I had the idea of getting her stuffed-animal mini party hats, the decision was made. It was probably the first and last party we would throw her where she didn't really know what was going on or have a say in what she wanted.

Steve's family came round, and my dad was there too (after I'd sent him home to put a shirt on – what is it with dads?!), and Aunty Jen, Aunty Amber and Uncle Matt had come down all the way from Edinburgh. I think because I had a big cry the morning of her actual birthday, I was fine when we all sang her happy birthday song. It was a day filled with joy. I was a bit worried about her nap schedule and needing to get her to sleep with a house full of people, but she had a huge nap in the morning before people came. It was like she knew, and another reminder that everything really does work out.

Conclusion
Finding Your Village

One of the most important things I've taken away from the past year is that mums are not supposed to do this on their own. You need support, whatever that may look like. Family, friends, new friends, neighbours – it can be anyone that you can talk to. My village made me more confident, and actually allowed me to learn my biggest lesson: trusting my gut.

I listened to the mums: my mum, her mum, my friends. These people were my village without me even realising they were. My midwife, Laura, held my hand through the whole journey. She was there from when I first found out I was pregnant, and she was there in the operating theatre when Billie was born – seeing her face made me feel like everything was going to be OK, and that's what your village should be for you too. As well as messaging Laura constantly, I also had my two best friends, Jo and Charlie, who I used as my own personal search engine. Watching them become mums and then becoming one myself made me feel like an awful person for not being there enough when they had their wee ones! There was so much I didn't know!

What really did feel like gaining a village physically was meeting all the mums in the antenatal classes. We were all at exactly the same stage, with a few weeks' difference between us, and all absolutely terrified! Ulrika and Rhiannon became my closer friends out of the group, and I can't imagine what I would have done without hearing they were also going through the same thing I was. This is what you need – and if any new grandmas or newly designated mum-friends (who have been through it before) are reading this and wondering how they can help: encourage the new mum in your life to build their village with mums who are at a similar stage to them.

I experienced this with Sara, a mum-to-be in our group who was six weeks behind me. I became the person she spoke to about what was going to happen. Never in a million years did I think I would be the one giving advice on babies any time soon, but here I was. I've known Sara since we were eleven, and she was one of the first friends I made when I moved to Scotland. Who would have thought that we would have been pregnant at the same time, and later taking our girls to get their feet painted on a mug.

I've learnt that in order to take care of your baby, you have to also take care of yourself. You may not be the number-one priority anymore in your life, but you still *are* a priority. My granny thinks we have it a lot easier now and, compared to some of her experiences, to an extent we do. Access to information can be immediate, and there are toys to keep a pram rocking, nursing bras that clip on and off. One of the biggest differences from Granny's time, though, is having a village ready-made, waiting for you, ready to share information. Having your family living on the same road or even in the same city is now not our normal. I'm very aware of how lucky I am to have moved to the same area as my mum, and to have Steve's family close too, so they can not only watch Billie grow up, but also spend time with her. We are doing it so differently to generations before us. I think this is mainly because of the insanely high expectations we have of women now, so we need to give ourselves a bit more credit and allow ourselves a break from the idea of having it all. My idea of what 'having it all' actually looks like changes daily. From writing a chapter of this book to baking a cake for Billie's birthday, it's not a balance but a juggling act.

Hearing my granny's stories about living in her one-bedroom flat, and my mum's story of having to go back to work three months after I was born, has made me realise how lucky I am. I'm only able to be the mum I am because of their sacrifices and everything they've taught me. There's a huge understanding and empathy I now feel for them both that appeared when I had Billie. The biggest lesson I learnt from them is to be patient with being a mum. There's such pressure for babies to reach their next steps from everyone around you, it seems, and it can often feel like, with every milestone, you have to throw out what you just learnt, and start anew! When they start to sit up, they'll be crawling next, and you won't ever get to sit down. 'Everything is temporary' is something I think every mum who has just given birth should get permanently tattooed.

I felt there was definitely a view that, when I became a mum, I'd know immediately know what to do. I'd know exactly what my baby was thinking, what they needed, why they were crying, and if they were too hot or too cold. The idea that the instant you give birth, you download vast amounts of information and now know *everything* is one that sets us all up to fail.

It took a long while for me to learn to listen not just to those around me, but to my intuition as well. This is the ultimate lesson I learnt, and the one which I hope readers will take from the book the most. If you're a mum already – or a grandma, even – I hope you will also take this away as the one thing to share with any new mum in your life.

I never felt like I lost my identity when I became a mum, but I did lose my autonomy. I can't access who I was a year ago, even, and remember what I was like before Billie, but I have no bad feelings about that. My time is no longer my own, and the ability to exist without every move being orchestrated is over! Feeding, naps, nappy changes and the simplest outings require planning and way more effort than you'll be used to – but that's OK too. When you do get a moment – when they're sleeping or with someone you trust – you're doing chores, catching up on sleep or running errands (that are usually all linked to them too!). Your switch is always 'on'. The mental load is something your partner will never really get, however lovely they are. The only people who do understand, in my experience, are other mums who have either gone through it before or are in the trenches with you. Lean on them! Be in this new world together. They'll have your back when you need a moment to breathe.

The most important thing to remember throughout everything is that you're going to be fine. You're equipped to do this, and all the power is within you. Your mum had it when having you, your granny had it, her mum had it, and so did her mum before her. There's a lot of noise out there, and it's so easy to get sucked into the world of social media and become disconnected from how natural this part of life is. You'll learn to sift through all the advice yourself and find your own way through this journey. Drown out all the noise, trust the people around you and, most importantly, learn to trust yourself.

For My Daughter

Dear Billie,

I get it now. My mum said that the minute I was born, something clicked, and holding me in the hospital for the first time, she realised that this was what 'it' was all about. She would always say this when talking about me to her friends, or in interviews in magazines, and I always rolled my eyes, literally or figuratively. I just never understood how something that seemed so normal, like having a baby, could change a person's outlook on life so completely.

It's such a cliché, but I still can't believe you're here. Everyone always says how fast time goes when you have a baby, but time for me, in our first year together in particular, just didn't exist. I can vividly remember being in bed with you, when you'd only sleep on me, watching reality TV on my iPad – and then time just jumped to you shoving baby pancakes into your mouth. Watching you grow up into the happiest (and cheekiest!) little monkey in the world has been the best thing that's ever happened to us. I have no idea what we did before you. (Apart from sleep!)

If babies are in your future, I hope it's easier for you than it was for me. You were a dream baby, but I just couldn't

♡

see past the fog of no sleep and the anxiety I experienced. Whether it's me, or your dad, or your partner, or a doctor, I hope you feel like you can talk about how you're feeling and get lots of help if and when you need it.

God knows what gadgets there'll be! Once, when I was breastfeeding from one boob and had a silicone pump on the other to collect the letdown milk, my mum (your granny) was astounded. She remembered feeding from one boob, too, and the other just leaking away – there were no such thing as breast pads, so she'd go through hundreds of T-shirts a day. There are pictures of my mum pregnant, and when I was born, of her wearing her trusty tartan dressing gown, or a house coat, as her great-granny Kelly used to say, and I don't think she took it off for the first two years of my life.

The main piece of advice I want to pass on, regardless of whether there are babies in the picture for you, is to not be too hard on yourself. You have to be kind and give yourself a break. If you do become a mother, remember that women have been doing this for years, but that you will find your own way. It'll be different from how it was for me, for my mum, and for her mum, too.

I want you to be able to talk to me about anything, just like I can with my mum. If we have just a fraction of the relationship I have with her, we'll be the best team ever. Whenever I send my mum a picture of you first thing in the morning, we always say to each other that you get more beautiful every day.

The most common thing people said to me when I was pregnant, and in the first few weeks, then months of your life, was how quickly time goes. One minute you're in

♡

my arms, and the next you'll be off to school, then uni, then getting married. I went against the advice of enjoying every minute and just loved (and still love!) watching you grow. I felt quite guilty, always looking to the next thing, like taking you swimming for the first time, getting you your first pair of shoes, seeing your first tooth come in. People say to enjoy the moment and that I'll miss you being so small, but every day, watching you do something different is such a blessing.

When we got past the newborn stage, you were the smiliest wee thing. When you started giggling, everyone would always say to me that you were just the happiest baby they'd ever seen. If I had you in your pram or carrier facing out to the world, people would stop me and say how beautiful your wee happy face was. I am in no way in denial about how cheeky you will be, though. From refusing bedtime to being a moody teenager, this is written in the stars – and we have all of that to look forward to. If you do have babies of your own, I'll be there, the same way my mum was when you were days old and I needed help washing my hair, putting body lotion on my legs because I couldn't bend down, and checking my scar to see if it was OK. I'll be there like she was, when she slept next to me and helped with night feeds when I was so ill from mastitis, or needed a lie-in.

When your dad and I got together, we would always say, 'Love you more than anything.' He said it when he proposed to me when I was six months pregnant with you, and we've kept the tradition going by saying it to you every night when you (eventually) go to sleep.

♡

    I can't wait to see you become even more of a wee person. If I get any prouder of you than I am now, I might combust as you get older.

    Love you more than anything,

Mummy x

♡

For My Mum

Dear Mum,

I can't comprehend that how I feel about Billie is how you felt about me. The two of us constantly ask each other now, 'What did we do before Billie?', and my answer nine times out of ten is 'sleep'. She has brought everyone so much joy, but I can really see how happy she's made you.

I need to give you the biggest thank you, not just for me, but also for Billie. When I was pregnant, I was looking at nurseries for her to go to and researching nannies, but the minute she was born, I didn't want her out of my sight. I trust you completely with her, which is something I didn't realise would be so hard to do.

Writing this book has made both of us realise how similar we are as mums, and just how similar I was as a baby to Billie! We stopped breastfeeding at the same time, Billie waves by clasping her fist just like I did, and we both slept with our bum in the air.

Sometimes, when it's just the three of us, life feels easier. Maybe it's because I'm being mothered too when you're there, but I also think I just feel more confident when you're around. When Billie was born and you

♡

talked about it on the show, you said I had really taken to motherhood and, at that point, I couldn't have disagreed more. I was all over the place – hormonal, boobs leaking, bleeding, with a tiny baby who depended on me. If I didn't have you present as much as you were, nearly setting up a camp in the hallway of our flat, I definitely wouldn't have had the same recovery. You were always worried about overstepping, but Steve and I genuinely loved your help.

You've shown me that motherhood challenges and changes everything, but essentially simplifies everything too. There is nothing more important to me now than Billie and making her happy. The best way I can do this, which you showed me, is just by being there. I don't remember it because I was about four, but I was Mary in the nativity play when you worked at TalkRadio, and you said you couldn't say what was on the show you missed that day and who you would have interviewed, but you remember every second of seeing me on stage for the first time.

With my childhood, there was never any pressure to be someone or do something a certain way, but there was always a focus on happiness. At parents' evening, you and Dad were not too bothered about my grades, but you told me the first question you would ask my teachers was if I had friends and if I was happy. This is definitely something I'll do with Billie and something I'm so grateful to you for doing for me.

You've always said to me, 'I'm not your friend, I'm your mum.' It's a relationship that's hard to explain but since becoming a mum, I'm starting to understand it.

♡

The unconditional love is all-consuming, and what I've come to realise is that you're a mum too, but at a different stage. Now you're a granny, you also have a whole new beginning. Seeing how cheeky Billie is, it's going to be a lot of fun . . . !

If Billie and I have half the relationship you and I do, we'll be all right.

Love,

Rosie

I Wish I'd Known...

FIRST TRIMESTER: Things I wish I'd known . . .

- The term 'morning sickness' is absolute bollocks – I felt nauseous from the second I woke up to the second I got to sleep. For me, I didn't actually throw up this whole time, but I definitely wanted to. I also felt so sick after taking my pre-natal vitamins, and had to remind myself about wanting a healthy baby.
- On that note, take pre-natal vitamins the minute you find out you're expecting. I waited until my first GP appointment because I wanted advice from a real-life doctor on which were best.
- Insomnia is real. Everything I'd heard about 'getting your sleep now before the baby comes' is a lie. I don't think I've had a full night's sleep without needing a wee or not being able to get to sleep without going over and over all the things that could go wrong.
- Limit tuna. Tuna pasta is my absolute go-to when it comes to comfort food, but because it has a higher level of mercury than other fish, it's not best to have a lot of it

– something I didn't know, and I had it twice in one week (oops).
- Put your snack of choice by your bed, because you need to eat the minute you wake up. I told my midwife in the first appointment that ginger biscuits were really helping me, and she said that you can either reach for ginger or mint as your remedy.
- Buy an anti-sickness bracelet and some foldable sick bags to shove in your bag.
- Get a pregnancy pillow – you don't need to start sleeping on your side until twenty-eight weeks, but I got one super early so I could get into the practice of being on my side. I've always slept cuddling another pillow or having it between my legs (which my friend Alex says is a sign of sexual frustration), but it was a game-changer when this tube the length of the bed arrived.
- If you're planning to get pregnant and it doesn't catch you off-guard, there are a few things I would advise:
  - Get a good relationship with your facialist, massagist, etc. A lot of beauticians won't touch a pregnant lady in her first trimester, but I was eight weeks when I had my facial booked and didn't know this was a rule. Luckily, I'd been seeing Jules for over a year, so she knows me and my skin, always uses natural products and was super helpful about what products I could use.
  - Same for hairdressers: if you have someone you always see, you'll feel way more comfortable asking for them to use natural products when you've dropped the pregnancy bomb.
- Don't use cream or oil on your stomach before a scan.

I Wish I'd Known . . .

SECOND AND THIRD TRIMESTER: Things I wish I'd known . . .

- Being angry is totally normal. I was gasping for a fight. Not anything bad or someone saying something to me, but more the opportunity to stand up for someone else.
- Carry tissues with you everywhere, because anything and everything will make you cry.
- Enjoy it – in the first trimester, you can't tell anyone, and in the third trimester you're too uncomfortable to do anything.
- Don't read before bed, especially birth research, as you'll likely not get to sleep with your mind racing.
- Symptoms come back with a vengeance, and there are some new ones too (I couldn't stand the air freshener we had in the car, and the diffusers we had at home felt like they had been poured down my throat).
- Learn about Braxton Hicks and actual contractions – what the difference is and when to get help if you think you might actually be in labour.
- If you're pregnant in the summer, dip two hand towels in cold water and freeze them to cool yourself down.
- Men start to nest, too – Steve ordered a leaf blower and a pressure washer so the stairs going into our basement flat wouldn't be a 'hazard'.
- One thing people told me about the hospital was to bring a fan in case it gets too hot, and to take a lot of layers. I ended up being in the hospital gowns, and then big oversized shirts I got from Markies. I wasn't ready to wear trousers or any kind of garment that went over my waist.

MOTHER TO MOTHER

A YEAR ON: Things I wish I'd known . . .

- Children don't thrive in perfection – they thrive in safety, security, consistency and love.
- Never trust a fart.
- If you buy into the airbrushed, anodyne, parenting-is-a-breeze content that is drenching your social media feeds, you are setting yourself up to fail.
- If you think you're failing, talk to yourself as if you were your best friend (or call or message your real-life best friend demanding words of reassurance – if they are a real friend, they won't even blink).
- Celebrate unwritten milestones – getting a new bra, going for a wee by yourself for the first time.
- Everything's a phase – GOOD AND BAD.
- Be kind to yourself.
- You think this is the way it's always going to be, but you will get your body and your life back, just in a very new and different way.
- You'll be in survival mode for most of the year, and will want to have a bit of control, so find the things you can do and don't set yourself up for failure from the beginning!
- Use any free time to nurture yourself; the house can wait.
- If you feel like having a big cry, have a big cry.

Acknowledgements

I decided to write this book three weeks before I gave birth. My friend Amber had given me a diary as a gift after I told her I was pregnant, and I really wanted to do something with all the notes I'd started to write down. Writing is always something I have loved, but I never thought I could make a career out of it. Without her buying that diary for me, and without her incredibly supportive friendship in general, none of this would be possible. Three weeks before Billie was due to come into the world, I had a very casual chat with my now-agent and friend Carly Cook, who believed in what I wanted to do. I couldn't have done this without her, and I can't thank her enough for everything she's done (including babysitting so I could get some words down!). Carly also introduced me to my book editor, Beth Eynon, who I've been so unbelievably lucky to work with on this. A total pro and so reassuring with everything.

I desperately need to thank my midwife Laura. She made sure I had the right care during and after pregnancy, and got me the support I needed, so the words 'thank you' will never be enough.

MOTHER TO MOTHER

I think I actually have two villages. All the mums I knew before Billie, and all those that became mums after me. I need to thank Hayley, who I met when I was five months pregnant, for showing me pictures of your birth and giving me a much better understanding of what would happen. Bronagh, who gave me my pregnancy belt and still keeps giving me the best tips with Billie. Kait, who introduced me to the world of teething powder, I owe you my life! Charlie and Jo, who I wish I had met sooner. I'd like to say thank you to you both – and apologise for messaging you in the wee hours for something I could have looked up. Hearing it from you, who I trust so much, was invaluable. Your babies are older than Billie, and this will never end, so I hope you're prepared for that!

I need to thank Sara and her gorgeous girl Willa for being Billie's best friend. Sending links of clothes for our girls to each other is one of my favourite ways to spend an evening, and you've been such a huge support in our first year of being mums. Another school friend, Ruth, helped me so much with her advice. You're the strongest woman I know, and Fred is so lucky to have you.

I'd like to also thank Ulrika and Rhiannon for their friendship, and for letting me share their stories in the book. The two of you are complete superhumans for everything you've gone through, and I thank God the timing all worked with our pregnancies so we met each other at antenatal class.

My best friends from school, Alex and Jen, whom I speak to every day – I still have Alex's Malteser traybake stain on our rocking chair from when I was glued to it for cluster feeding, and it constantly reminds me how lucky I am to

Acknowledgements

have you. Billie is obsessed with the two of you, and I'm so grateful you're still putting up with me after all these years.

A big thanks to both my dad and my partner – 'the Steves' – for their support and for letting me be so honest about them and their experiences too. I'd also like to thank my great-aunt Josephine for letting me share her experience of motherhood and for always giving us a giggle.

My biggest thank you, of course, goes to my granny and my mum for allowing me to share their stories of motherhood in this book. You've both always been the biggest inspiration, and none of this could have happened without your help.

RAISING READERS
Books Build Bright Futures

Dear Reader,

We'd love your attention for one more page to tell you about the crisis in children's reading, and what we can all do.

Studies have shown that reading for fun is the **single biggest predictor of a child's future life chances** – more than family circumstance, parents' educational background or income. It improves academic results, mental health, wealth, communication skills, ambition and happiness.[1]

The number of children reading for fun is in rapid decline. Young people have a lot of competition for their time. In 2024, 1 in 10 children and young people in the UK aged 5 to 18 did not own a single book at home.[2]

Hachette works extensively with schools, libraries and literacy charities, but here are some ways we can all raise more readers:

- Reading to children for just 10 minutes a day makes a difference
- Don't give up if children aren't regular readers – there will be books for them!
- Visit bookshops and libraries to get recommendations
- Encourage them to listen to audiobooks
- Support school libraries
- Give books as gifts

There's a lot more information about how to encourage children to read on our website: **www.RaisingReaders.co.uk**

Thank you for reading.

---

[1] OECD, '21st-Century Readers: Developing Literacy Skills in a Digital World', 2021, https://www.oecd.org/en/publications/21st-century-readers_a83d84cb-en.html

[2] National Literacy Trust, 'Book Ownership in 2024', November 2024, https://literacytrust.org.uk/research-services/research-reports/book-ownership-in-2024